Do-it-yourself

Credit File

Jill Stevens

LAW PACK™
GUIDE

Published by
Law Pack Publishing Limited
10-16 Cole Street
London SE1 4YH
www.lawpack.co.uk

Credit File Guide by Jill Stevens

© Law Pack Publishing Limited 1999
ISBN: 1-898217-77-7
All rights reserved.

Printed in the United Kingdom.

Important facts

This Law Pack Guide contains information and advice on the law as it applies to consumer credit and credit reference agencies. This Guide is for use throughout the United Kingdom.

The information it contains has been carefully compiled from professional sources, but its accuracy is not guaranteed, as laws and regulations may change or be subject to differing interpretations.

Neither this nor any other publication can take the place of a solicitor on important legal matters. As with any legal matter, common sense should determine whether you need the assistance of a solicitor rather than relying solely on the information and forms in this Law Pack Guide.

LAW PACK GUIDE

Table of contents

Introduction

It's a way of life

Credit comes in many different guises. Most people would recognise credit as a cash loan or a mortgage from a bank or a building society, or being able to pay for goods from a shop in instalments.

Credit cards are obviously a form of credit, whether you pay off the balance in part or in full each month. Perhaps not so obviously, your mobile phone agreement is a credit agreement, and so are your dealings with mail order catalogues if you pay after you have received the goods. And if you rent your television, that's a credit arrangement, too.

In the past ten years the use of credit has increased to the point where most adults – in fact about 75% of the UK population – use some form of credit as part of their day to day lives.

We now take credit for granted. Lenders have made the way we can apply for credit as easy as possible. They have simplified their forms and we can even ask for a loan over the phone. But how many of us read the 'terms and conditions' of our credit deals? How many of us really understand what we are agreeing to when we decide to pay for goods in 'easy payments'? How many of us bother to check the details of our credit card accounts?

Applying for credit may be easy, and consumers may be protected by a raft of laws and codes of conduct to make sure they are not taken advantage of, but when you take out any form of loan, you are entering into a contract with the lender, and you should always make sure that you do understand your part of the bargain.

Most household items are usually available on credit. Fridges, vacuum cleaners, cookers, washing machines and tumble driers – many of us wouldn't have a kitchen filled with the latest appliances if it wasn't for the fact that we are able to pay for them month by month rather than in one lump sum.

Upstairs and down, most houses are evidence of how the use of credit has raised our standard of living. The carpets, the replacement double-glazed windows, the central heating, even in some cases the pictures on the walls, the limited edition plates on the dresser and the books and videos on the shelves are the result of a credit deal.

Outside, we may still be paying for the garden shed and the green-house. And almost certainly the car in the road, in the drive or in the garage is only partly ours because we will have bought it with the help of a loan.

And, of course, credit usually provides the actual roof over our heads. The house itself, if you 'own' rather than rent, will be the subject of a mortgage – usually the biggest credit deal any of us enter into.

When you consider how dependent the average family has become on credit, it clearly makes sense to learn a little about how the world of credit works. Getting credit may sometimes seem easy, but in fact the way credit operates can sometimes be complicated.

Consumers have rights and the UK has laws which are designed to protect consumers. Credit grantors are increasingly conducting their businesses in accordance with a range of codes of conduct which make it difficult for the consumer to be cheated. But with rights come responsibilities. If things go wrong, it is rarely any use complaining that you didn't understand what you were agreeing to. It is up to every one of us to make sure that we do understand. And to make sure that these things are explained to us.

Chapter

Household goods on credit

Highlight

Don't take out a loan for longer than you need to. Work out the difference in the final price between a long-term loan with small repayments and a shorter one with larger repayments.

There are many different ways in which we use credit. The most everyday method is when buying goods, particularly household appliances, in a shop. If you're buying goods like these on credit – anything from carpets to a fridge or a camcorder – always ask the following questions:

How much would you pay if you bought the goods outright?

Find out the cash price and check that they are not cheaper somewhere else, particularly if you're being offered a 0% finance deal.

How much will you pay in total if you buy the goods on credit?

Add up all the monthly repayments and check how much you'll have paid by the time you've finished the deal. Compare that to the cash price. Is the difference worth the benefit of having the goods now rather than later?

Do you really need credit?

Must you have the goods now or could you wait a while? Could you wait long enough to save up the cash price and avoid having to pay interest on credit?

How long will you be paying for the goods?

Are your personal circumstances secure enough for you to know that you'll be able to keep up the repayments for that long? Do you have a choice of how much to pay and how long to take out the agreement for? Don't take out a loan for longer than you need to. Work out the difference in the final price between a long-term loan with small repayments and a shorter one with larger repayments.

Exactly what sort of deal is it?

Are you being offered credit, or hire purchase?

Can you end the deal early if you can afford it? Or is there a penalty clause for settling up early?

Is this a fixed interest arrangement, or can the store or finance company backing the deal vary the rate, which would mean your repayments could go up or down?

Do you have to pay a deposit, or pay for insurance?

Is the shop's credit a better deal than buying the goods with a small loan from the bank or building society or putting them on your credit card?

Can you really afford it?

Get it in writing

If the price of the goods you are buying is more than £50, the shop must give you a written quotation.

It's always a good idea to ask for this. If something is written down it's usually easier to understand and you can check exactly what you are expected to pay, how and when, before you say 'yes' or 'no'.

Don't be scared to say 'no'

If the deal is not what you want, or you decide you can do without the goods, or to look elsewhere for a better deal, never be scared to say 'no, thank you'. Don't be worried about offending the sales person, or be tempted to impress him or her. People actually respect someone who can sensibly say 'no' or who is obviously bright enough to want to think about a deal before signing on the dotted line. Never agree to a credit deal until you are absolutely sure it meets your needs.

Special offers

Everyone loves a bargain – and there really are some good deals around if you hunt for them. But don't be tempted into parting with your hard-earned cash simply because the price tag tells you this is something you can't afford to miss. Find out for yourself if this is true. And remember that a bargain for one person can be a waste of money for another. It's only a good deal if you really want or need the goods on offer.

Interest free credit, or deals which allow you to 'buy now, pay later' – sometimes much later, even more than a year away – sound wonderful. But all the same rules apply. So don't be tempted now and find yourself really paying – for your mistake – later. Ask yourself:

- Do I need this or does it just look like a good deal?

- Can I really afford it?

- If I can't afford it now, why do I think I'll be able to afford it later?

■ Will I really get that bonus at work?

■ Is my partner right now planning to spend the windfall we're expecting on something else?

■ Does the final price I'll pay mean this is really a bargain?

■ Can I trust myself to save up each month so that I can pay for this eventually?

Just in case

You will often be offered a credit deal which includes insurance. This is designed to help you if you find yourself unable to pay, perhaps because you are made redundant or you fall ill for a long time.

While it is sensible to make sure you have planned for a rainy day, sometimes this insurance is not cheap. And you must check exactly what you are covered for. For example, you will probably find that if you leave your job and can't get another, you won't be covered, because you will have created that situation yourself. You may also find yourself still having to find the money for repayments if your partner is unable to earn. He or she may not be included in the insurance, even though you are taking their wages into consideration when deciding whether or not you can afford the goods.

Always check that you need the insurance and whether the credit is available without it. You might even be able to find a cheaper way of insuring your credit deals with a separate policy from another insurance company.

Satisfaction guaranteed

The deal you're being offered might also include an extended guarantee or warranty.

Most new goods are guaranteed when you first buy them, usually for about a year. But hopefully you'll be using them for longer than that. So again, it's sensible to plan for trouble, especially if you're buying something that you or a friend could not easily repair yourself if it went wrong – for example a television or a computer.

These extended guarantees can cover the cost of anything from minor repairs, parts and labour to just major faults and parts only. Check what you're being asked to pay for. How long does the extended guarantee last? Is it renewable at the same terms? And find out if there is a cheaper way of getting the same benefits, for example through the manufacturer rather than the shop, or through your household insurance policy. Is the credit deal available without the guarantee?

Highlight

Always check that you need the insurance and whether the credit is available without it.

Make sure that the cost of the extended guarantee is worth what you might have to pay out for repairs. And find out if the goods you are buying are likely to go wrong. Guarantees rarely last for ever and you don't want to find that yours runs out just at the time the appliance starts showing the signs of age. The shop may not be keen to tell you, but there are magazines and consumer organisations which list this sort of thing and research the expected life of various goods and what are the best buys.

You shouldn't be buying an expensive item on impulse. It's always best to have checked out what's available and what's value for money.

And remember that under the Sale of Goods Act 1979 (as amended) you do not need a guarantee to get a replacement or your money back for goods which are faulty from the start.

One at a time

Beware of taking on too much credit at one time. Each arrangement, individually, may genuinely be a great deal. You could have found yourself some real bargains. And the goods you are buying might really be things you genuinely need. But add all your repayments together and you might be in for a shock.

Common danger times include when you're moving into a new home, or planning a new venture, like working from home, which involves the need for new equipment.

It is always a temptation to make a fresh start. You may not want to have to make do with the same three piece suite that you had in the old house. This may seem an ideal time to replace the cooker which has a knob missing and which looks shabby in your new fitted kitchen, or the washing machine which has rattled ever since that shirt button went missing.

You may feel that you'd work much more efficiently from home with a new desk and an impressive phone-cum-fax-cum-answering machine.

And all this may well be true. You'll certainly be able to find all that you need in the shops and undoubtedly everything you'd like to buy will be available on credit. But all of us have to make do and mend at some stage in our lives, and periods of change are the flash points when we may need to face this fact and be extra careful not to take on too much credit.

Most stores, indeed most lenders, do try to make sure that they are not allowing you to overcommit (more about how they do that later). For a start they want to make sure you will eventually pay for any goods you're buying from them on credit. But in the end it is up to consumers to take responsibility for their actions. So always make sure that any fresh start is not the forerunner to money troubles down the line.

This doesn't work

If there is something wrong with the goods you have bought on credit, you must not stop the repayments. Go back to the shop or supplier and ask for the goods to be replaced or the faults repaired. And keep a note of when and to whom you complain. If possible put it in writing. If things are not sorted out to your satisfaction, seek advice through a solicitor or the Citizens Advice Bureau but don't stop paying until legally advised to do so.

If you've bought the goods with credit from a finance company rather than the store itself, or with your credit card, then you might be able to claim against the lender. You might also find that the goods are insured for a certain length of time, too. Contact the credit company to find out where you stand.

Chapter

Mortgages:
the roof over our heads

Highlight

Even if you are making the deal through a broker, or an adviser – independent or otherwise – you should always check every aspect of the mortgage and understand exactly what you are agreeing to.

For most people, arranging a mortgage so that they can buy their own home is the most important financial deal they'll ever make. It is important because people invest a huge amount, not just financially but also emotionally, in having the security of a place to live. So your well-being and probably that of your family can be at stake when you decide to take out a mortgage.

Because mortgages inevitably involve thousands of pounds, we should be extra vigilant before we sign, but ironically sometimes we take less care over a mortgage than we would over a small credit deal. Some people shop around for a good deal on a CD player and wouldn't dream of paying £100 more than they could afford for a second-hand car, but when it comes to the mortgage they get blinded by the row of 0s and lose all sense of reality.

You are unlikely to be granted a mortgage that you cannot afford to repay. While the consumer is expected to take extra care over such a large sum of money, so the lender will be making sure that this is a loan they can afford to grant. But you should never hand over responsibility for such a huge decision to a third party. Even if you are making the deal through a broker, or an adviser – independent or otherwise – you should always check every aspect of the mortgage and understand exactly what you are agreeing to.

Mortgages last a long time, usually about 25 years. For the whole of that period you will be making regular repayments. Unless you have a fixed rate mortgage, these repayments can vary, according to the interest rate being charged by your lender. They can go up or down, but it is always best to assume that 'up' will be the norm. Most people pay their mortgage by direct debit or standing order from their bank account. If the money is not there when the mortgage company tries to claim it, you can be in trouble with your bank as well as your mortgage grantor. If you fail to keep up repayments, for whatever reason, you could lose your home, either by having to sell or because the mortgage company decides to repossess the property.

When you consider the enormity of all this for most people, it becomes clear that we should spend some time and effort getting to grips with this area of our lives.

Events beyond our control

There is, of course, a limit to how careful we can be. None of us would have bought houses in the late 1980s if we could have foreseen that the interest rate would rise so high, and the value of property would sink so low, that we were left with mortgages worth more than the value of our homes. Many people found themselves in this situation, with what is called 'negative equity'. In other words they owed more on their home than they could raise by selling it.

Many people held on, paid the higher repayments and eventually the price of their property went up again and the interest rate fell. Some negotiated with their lenders and made reduced payments and managed to hold on that way. But some found they could not afford any repayments, particularly if their jobs were affected by what was a recession bordering on a depression. They became victims by being made redundant. Many people came to grief and a few are still sorting out the mess they were left in.

If you had negative equity, selling up was not often an option. If you couldn't repay the difference, you were stuck and repossessions reached an all-time high. Mortgage companies had to recoup their losses somehow and while they were mostly reluctant to take this course of action, they were left with few alternatives.

This situation that many of us remember, caused by events, political and economic, outside the influence of ordinary people, should nevertheless serve as a warning to all of us contemplating taking on a mortgage. Those who did not feel the effect of the recession were those homeowners whose mortgages were so old that inflation over the years meant their repayments were now comparatively low, or those who had been prudent and who had arranged mortgages with repayments that they could very easily afford, even in difficult circumstances.

How much to borrow?

The amount that you can borrow will usually be determined by the lender and will be based on your annual salary. Most companies will lend you about three times your annual gross wage or, in the case of a joint mortgage, then they will offer about two and a half times your combined annual incomes. It is difficult to be precise about this, because some lenders will offer you more, some will offer you less.

Highlight

A mortgage is a long-term commitment and it pays to know yourself. It is not always what you spend your money on now, but what you will spend it on in the future that needs to be taken into account here.

It is up to the lender to decide the top limit they will offer you. But there is no law which says you have to borrow all of this. Only you really know how much you can afford to repay, or indeed how much of your income you want to devote to owning your home.

This is a very personal decision. Some people decide that this is the most important purchase they will ever make, and that they will go without other things in order to be able to afford to pay for it. If they keep to their decision to forgo holidays and other treats for a few years, and they get the wage rises that mean the mortgage repayments are no longer such a huge percentage of their income, then they end up with what they wanted – a more expensive home.

But many people decide not to take that risk. They know that they want to go on holiday at least once a year, that they will need or want to spend their money on other things for the home, or on redecorating, or simply on regular treats such as meals out or trips to the cinema. And so they take all this into account when deciding how much they can afford to borrow.

A mortgage is a long-term commitment and it pays to know yourself. It is not always what you spend your money on now, but what you will spend it on in the future that needs to be taken into account here. And while, as we discussed earlier, some events are almost impossible to predict, we can all work out the effect of a gradual rise in the interest rate. Calculate what you would have to pay if it went up by 1 or 2%. Because it might. Ask the mortgage grantor, or the broker, to work this out for you and write it down. Also find out if the mortgage grantor is likely to extend the period of the mortgage, rather than insist on the higher payments, if things do get sticky.

Sometimes it is sensible to take one step at a time, starting with a mortgage that you can very easily afford and moving on when the time is right and more money is available to buy a more expensive property with a more expensive mortgage.

And don't forget that most mortgage lenders will not part with any money until they're sure you could repay them in the event of a disaster. With nearly all mortgages, they will insist that you take out life insurance, in case you die, and that you insure the building you are buying against fire, storm or flood damage, subsidence and the like. This all costs money. Take it into account.

Because they're lending you a large amount of money, mortgage companies will ask you for a fairly detailed account of where your money comes from and how you spend it. Take this opportunity to sort these things out in your own mind. Be realistic when budgeting. Remember that if you buy a house, you will need to put something by for unexpected, as well as usual, repairs. You should budget for maintenance, which might include large items, for example a new roof, as well as the more ordinary, such as redecorating.

All of the above should be in your mind when deciding what sort of mortgage you want, as well as how much you need to borrow, and what type of repayment suits you best.

Repayment mortgages

With a repayment mortgage you are repaying the amount you have borrowed, plus the interest, over the lifetime of the mortgage. If you take out a 25-year repayment mortgage and you keep up the repayments, you will spend 25 years paying off the loan and paying the interest you're being charged on it. You will owe nothing and you will own your home outright at the end of the 25 years.

The amount of your repayments, and what they represent, will undoubtedly vary, though. Each monthly repayment will be partly for the amount you have borrowed – called the capital sum – and partly interest on this amount. The interest will be worked out each year and will be based on the amount of the capital sum you still owe.

So at the beginning of the mortgage, you will be paying more interest. Some mortgages are arranged so that all you pay is interest for the first year or two. But eventually you will be paying off some of the capital sum each month. And as the amount you owe goes down, so does the interest payable. But this doesn't mean you pay less, because as the amount of interest you pay goes down, the amount of your monthly repayment off the capital sum goes up. Eventually, towards the end of the mortgage term, your monthly repayments will consist of a small amount for interest, and the rest will be paying off the final thousand or so that you originally borrowed.

If you get into temporary financial difficulties, your mortgage company might agree to let you carry on paying that part of your monthly repayment which is interest, but stop paying that which is paying off the capital sum. But this is likely to be only a short-term arrangement, as the company will want all its money back eventually. And the difference an arrangement like this can make to the total you need to pay each month will vary depending on how long you've had the mortgage. If it's new, then as you can see from the explanation above, it might make very little difference to the amount you pay, as most of that will already be interest.

When working out how much you'll be paying out each month on a repayment mortgage, take into account that a condition of the mortgage will usually be that you have life insurance to the value of the loan. So add the monthly payments for this insurance to the monthly mortgage repayments (and don't forget buildings insurance). Mortgage companies do not actually want to own property, their business is lending money – if you die, they don't want your home, they want their money back. With life insurance the mortgage can be repaid in a lump sum if you die. Not only the lender but also your family benefits, because on your death the mortgage would be paid but the property would belong to whoever you leave it to, without any money being owed on it.

With joint mortgages, both lives are insured, so that the surviving partner can similarly pay off the mortgage and then own the home. Even if just one of you could afford alone to keep up the monthly mortgage repayments, this insurance will more than likely be required by the lender.

Endowment mortgages

If you take out an endowment mortgage, you don't pay off the capital sum until the mortgage comes to an end. What you pay each month is the interest on the total loan. Unlike with a repayment mortgage, where the capital sum goes down as you pay a little off each month, with an endowment mortgage the amount you owe stays the same. In other words the amount you are paying interest on, stays the same. So your monthly repayments will consist of interest only and will remain the same unless the interest rate changes – which is likely. And the whole of your repayment will be affected by any changes.

But at the end of the mortgage term, you still owe the capital sum you borrowed. And it will need to be repaid in full. This money comes from the maturity value of a life insurance endowment policy, which you will be required to take out at the same time as the mortgage.

The insurance company you take out the policy with will decide how much you need to pay in premiums each month to make sure you will receive the amount you have borrowed from the mortgage company at the end of the agreement. You will probably be able to choose which insurance company to take out a policy with, but you may be advised to deal with one chosen by your mortgage lender and you will certainly need to (and would be foolish not to) deal with a reputable company with a proven track record.

Highlight

If you take out an endowment mortgage, you don't pay off the capital sum until the mortgage comes to an end. What you pay each month is the interest on the total loan.

Taking out an endowment policy means you are saving up towards paying off the mortgage in a lump sum by investing in an insurance policy. It must be remembered, however, that no insurance company can guarantee how much you will receive when the policy matures. Everyone hopes that you will get back considerably more than you have invested, and that the value of the policy will go up all the time. But this cannot be relied upon. Insurance companies take your money and invest it in a huge variety of ways. Some investments prove more profitable than others and, although it is happily rare, some can even fail completely.

You should end up with at least enough to pay off the mortgage. And life insurance will be included so that the mortgage can be paid off early if you die, but you should regularly check what the policy is worth. The insurance company should advise you if your premiums need to be increased, but keep an eye on this yourself anyway by checking annual statements, to make sure you do not end up with less than you need when your mortgage term ends.

When working out how much an endowment policy will cost you, add the monthly interest payments to the monthly insurance premiums and, again, don't forget to add the cost of buildings insurance.

Other mortgages

There are other types of mortgages available. These can vary and different products are available at different times. The choice depends on what companies are offering and sometimes on what the government decides is acceptable. They will usually be similar to endowment mortgages, but will mean your money is invested differently. They are usually tied in with pension plans. A financial adviser will have details of everything on offer at the time you decide to enter the mortgage market.

It is always worth looking at fixed rate mortgages – which mean you pay interest at an agreed rate for a certain length of time. This could be for the life of the mortgage, or for a fixed term.

A mortgage which starts at a low interest rate and then, after an agreed period of time, reverts to the rate being charged by the lender at the time, can be a good way to help you get acclimatised to having a mortgage. But do calculate how much the repayments will ultimately be and that the increase won't come as too much of a shock.

Lenders should make all this clear to you, but they are allowed to highlight the lower rate as a selling point.

Cashback deals can be just what people need when they're moving house or taking out a mortgage for the first time. The lump sum can help you put your new home in order and if you use it for essential household repairs or maintenance, an extension, work in the garden or just for redecorating, you are probably increasing the value of your property as well as making life more comfortable for yourself. This has to be a sensible way to spend the cash.

It is not so wise to blow the cashback payment on a luxury which you wouldn't otherwise be able to afford. There is no such thing as a free lunch. Someone is actually paying for the cashback payment – and it's you. If you need a holiday, or want to buy something inessential, there may be a cheaper way than a cashback mortgage to pay for it, such as a short-term loan. This may also be a better way of obtaining ready cash to spend on essentials in your new home, too.

Always remember that mortgage grantors are not naive. They are in business to make money, so they are unlikely to offer you a deal that is unprofitable to them. And also remember that interest rates can go down as well as up. What looks like a really good fixed rate deal when the general interest rate is high, can turn out to be less of a bargain if the interest rate goes down to below what you've agreed to pay. You'll be tied to the higher rate.

Some deals truly are very good value, but you may need to shop around to find them. Lenders mix and match all of the above in order to attract custom. You have to work out what you want, what you need and what you can afford. A mortgage is actually a very personal thing. The advice you receive can be crucial.

The right mortgage

There is no easy way to find out which is the right mortgage for you. Generally, if you are looking for security above all else, then a repayment mortgage is straightforward – you borrow the money from one company, then you repay it, with interest, until it's paid off.

An endowment mortgage, or one that involves any form of investment, is more risky in that you are relying on someone else to make a profit for you. Your ability to repay the money you've borrowed depends on their investment decisions.

Both types of mortgage could well involve increased payments at some point down the line.

A pension-linked mortgage could be right for you if the other benefits involved are what you need. If in doubt, seek independent advice.

Highlight

Someone is actually paying for the cashback payment – and it's you. If you need a holiday, or want to buy something inessential, there may be a cheaper way than a cashback mortgage to pay for it, such as a short-term loan.

On the move and making changes

If you are thinking of moving and selling your house, you must first check that your mortgage makes this a sensible move. You may not want to move, but you may decide to look around for a better deal than the one you have. Or you may simply want or need to give up the mortgage altogether. So before you buy, check out the charges and penalties you would incur if you have to settle up earlier than planned.

Surprisingly, some lenders say that nearly one-third of endowment mortgages are surrendered in the first five years of the life of the policy. A variety of circumstances can be responsible, from redundancy to a bereavement or the breakdown of a relationship.

Whatever the situation, it is worth knowing that in general it is likely to cost you more to give up an endowment policy early than a repayment mortgage.

Always ask what you would be charged if you did have to back out of the agreement, even if you think it is unlikely. Terms will vary a lot from company to company. If you think this is a likely scenario, then always choose a company offering low charges and a high surrender value.

If you want to move, in simple terms, with a repayment mortgage, if the new value of your house is more than the amount you owe, you can pay off the mortgage and start again with another. You might even find you make a profit.

You can do the same with an endowment mortgage, but it's worth taking a close look at the endowment insurance policy involved. If it has been running for any length of time, you will have paid quite a lot into this investment already. Paying off the mortgage grantor does not mean you also have to cancel the endowment with the insurance company.

Always check whether or not you can transfer the policy, or have it altered, to enable you take out another investment-linked mortgage on another property. If this is not possible, it might still be worth your while continuing with the endowment, using it as a way of saving.

Your decision will have to be influenced, of course, by how much you can afford to pay out each month.

If you simply cancel the policy, or just stop paying the premiums, you will effectively lose all the money you've paid in so far, as well as being liable for any penalties – although it is true that the endowment policy will have served its purpose as an essential component of your original mortgage.

The best advice

There is no shortage of advice available when it comes to mortgages. Lenders themselves will steer you around the different products they have on offer. Estate agents often have a financial adviser on hand to help you explore all the options and will be able to tell you what deals the different companies are doing.

This advice ostensibly comes free, and it's true that you won't have to pay for it up front, but be aware that there may be a fine line between advice and a sales pitch. And you do indirectly pay for the advice, as the price of commission, or your adviser's salary, is all part of the deal you're doing.

If you're dealing with just one lender, you will learn about that company's products only. And you might be steered towards the deal that is flavour of the month because that's the product that company wants to sell right now.

You may think it wiser to use an adviser to help you shop around. But most financial advisers, even if they are not based on the premises, are employed by one of the financial institutions, be it a lender or an insurance company. Don't forget, even if you plump for a repayment mortgage, you'll need that life insurance. An adviser tied to one insurance company may well be able to offer you a range of mortgages from various companies, but when it comes to the insurance will only sell you a policy offered by his or her employer.

Some advisers are independent in that they are not tied to any one company. But they may depend solely on the commission paid to them by the companies their clients decide to do business with. They are obviously going to hope you choose a product which pays good commission. For example, higher commission is often paid on endowment policies than on straightforward life cover. And your adviser will hope you choose a company which generally pays them a good rate no matter which mortgage you pick.

There is really no such thing as an independent financial adviser, although it's true to say that some are more independent than others. It's also true that while the advice they give you could represent the best deal for them, it might also be the best deal for you, too. And financial advisers are now very strictly regulated. Insurance companies in particular had their fingers burned a few years ago and some are now paying the price – in hefty compensation – for the not-so-good advice given by some of their representatives.

Highlight

This advice ostensibly comes free, and it's true that you won't have to pay for it up front, but be aware that there may be a fine line between advice and a sales pitch.

Consumers are safer when seeking financial advice now than they were. It is your right to receive good advice. But carefully examine everything put your way. You may be shown more than you need, such as house contents cover or mortgage protection or health insurance. If you can afford them, they may all be a good idea in principle, but don't buy just because something's offered. There may be better deals available around the corner or indeed with a range of different companies. It may be tempting to put all your mortgage-associated finances with one firm – and it could be the best value. But make sure this is the case before you buy. If you don't you could find that the extras on each deal mount up to quite a large sum each month.

Always ask your adviser who they are employed by and find out what's in it for them. They won't be offended. And they'll know that they're dealing with someone who is on the ball.

If the adviser who introduces him or herself to you cannot offer you the independent choices you want, or you feel you are being pressured into taking a certain route, then find someone else or make enquiries yourself with all the different lenders.

Mortgage muddles

Because your home is at stake, if you have difficulty paying your mortgage it is crucial that you speak to the lender as quickly as you can. They really don't want to have to repossess the property and would much rather find a way of helping you get out of trouble. Lenders will often allow you to pay the interest on the mortgage only until you've sorted yourself out. Or they can make the term of the mortgage longer, which is another way of reducing the monthly repayments you have to make.

Those lenders who are in the mortgage business should belong to one or other of the trade associations, for example, the British Bankers' Association, the Building Societies' Association or the Council of Mortgage Lenders. And the Banking or Building Society Ombudsman can be asked to investigate if you feel you have been unfairly treated (see Appendix for details). The Ombudsman is an independent arbitrator appointed by the government to make decisions in the case of disputes between consumers and the companies they're dealing with. You must try to sort things out with the lender first, and then with the appropriate trade association.

Keep a record of all paperwork and conversations on the phone or in person, because if you cannot get satisfaction form the lender or their association then you can ask the Ombudsman to decide whether or not you have a justified grievance.

Chapter

Bank business

Although we may think of banks as primarily places where our hard-earned cash is kept safe, ready for us to use when we need to, one of the main areas of bank business is actually the lending of money and they offer a variety of forms of credit.

Going into the red

Overdrafts, especially if they are unauthorised, are usually an expensive way to get credit. But they can be a useful safety net, especially if you have direct debits and standing orders attached to your bank account but cannot always be sure of the exact date money will be paid in.

Going into the red without the bank's permission should always be avoided. When you open an account ask about overdraft facilities. You may be granted them immediately, or the bank may want you to operate the account for a certain length of time before they let you overdraw – because they want to see how you manage the account first.

When setting up an overdraft you will be told how much the bank will allow you to 'borrow', but – much like when you are deciding how much to borrow on a mortgage – you don't have to agree to the full amount. Work out how much you might need to cover any shortfall if your wages are paid late or if you suddenly lose your income. It might be a good idea to make sure that the mortgage and any essential bills can be paid.

Beware of seeing an overdraft as a licence to spend. Overdrawing by a little, in fact by as much as you can easily afford to repay the next month, is acceptable. Using an overdraft as a permanent way to make ends meet can be dangerous. You will usually pay interest and bank charges on an overdraft.

Overdrafts do not need to be subject to a credit agreement, but it is always wise to have written evidence of the arrangement, for example a letter from the bank stating your overdraft limit.

While there is usually no time limit on an overdraft you do eventually have to repay the amount. If your bank thinks it is in danger of losing its money it will ask you to do just that. For example, if you stop using the account, the bank could understandably become wary.

Leaving an overdraft on an account into which you are not paying money is dangerous because the amount overdrawn is not going down. In fact it is going up. You are charged interest on the outstanding

Highlight

Overdrafts do not need to be subject to a credit agreement, but it is always wise to have written evidence of the arrangement, for example a letter from the bank stating your overdraft limit.

amount. That interest is added to the original figure. The next month, that total becomes the outstanding amount on which you are charged interest. So each month the interest will be more. Eventually, and probably sooner than you think, you will be over your limit and liable to even higher and different charges. Banks do not wait very long before acting in this situation.

Bank loans

An ordinary bank loan is usually available only to existing bank customers. And you will be asked what you want to spend the money on. Typically it would be for a special holiday, a large item for the home, to pay for home improvements, or to buy a car or caravan. You should usually get the loan as long as you can show that it will be repaid.

It will be subject to an agreement which you will sign and will be regulated by the Consumer Credit Act 1974. The interest you pay will vary and can change during the life of the loan, depending on the rate at the time.

If the loan is for a substantial sum, the bank may ask for security. If you are a homeowner this will probably be a second charge on your property, in addition to the mortgage you probably already have.

If you fail to repay the loan, the bank can demand that you sell the property in order for it to recoup the money it has lent you.

Personal loans can be offered by banks to people who are not their customers as well as those who are. These loans are subject to a fixed rate of interest which you agree to when you make the deal. A personal loan, because it is usually unsecured, can be a more expensive way of getting credit than an ordinary loan.

Other bank credit

Banks offer many other forms of credit, including mortgages, and will readily provide you with brochures about all the services available.

They may offer current or cheque accounts which allow you to pay your bills when they become due, knowing that you may need to 'overdraw' when bills are higher, in the winter for example, but that things will even out in the summer when you use less fuel. Such an arrangement will probably involve you paying a set sum each month which is a twelfth of the total to be paid each year.

Budgeting in this way can be effective but you may have to pay a charge for such an account. And as most of the utilities, and most local authorities to whom you pay council tax, now allow you to pay your bills in regular instalments by direct debit or standing order, spreading the cost across the year, this type of bank account is less popular than it was.

Highlight

Hire purchase was at one time a very popular form of credit, but as more and more ways to obtain goods on credit have been developed, it is used much less these days.

Building on success

Building societies began life as institutions providing money specifically to pay for houses to be built, but gradually became mortgage and home loan specialists. Many building societies have now become banks and those that remain offer a range of credit and other services, including current accounts. But building societies are still best known for their mortgages and for top-up loans for which your home will usually be used as security. The rules detailed earlier about mortgages apply whether you obtain your mortgage from a building society or other lender.

The never never

Buying goods on hire purchase used to be known as the 'never never'. This was a dangerous misnomer, for credit obtained in this way in fact 'always always' had to be repaid.

Hire purchase was at one time a very popular form of credit, but as more and more ways to obtain goods on credit have been developed, it is used much less these days. It does still exist though, and sometimes people who are buying goods on hire purchase are unaware of the difference between this and a straightforward credit deal.

The difference, as the name suggests, is that the goods you have are not actually yours until you have finished paying for them. And then you officially have to exercise an 'option to purchase'.

If you fail to make regular payments, the supplier can repossess the goods and if they have been lost or damaged you will be liable to make good any loss. The supplier must send you official notice, before ending the agreement, though, and if you have already repaid more than a third of the total cost the supplier needs a court order to retrieve the goods. Even if you've paid less than a third, the supplier can only enter your home to collect the goods if you give permission. If you think it is worth asking for extra time to pay, you can yourself apply for a court order allowing you to do this.

What you do in this situation would depend very much on what the goods were and how much you needed them. If they were inessentials, it might be worth cutting your losses. If you had been made redundant, and the hire purchase concerned a car which you needed to search for a new job, it might be worth taking action. But avoid getting into this situation. It is always advisable to negotiate to alter or to end an agreement yourself, in other words to act before the supplier or lender needs to. If you think you are going to have difficulty making repayments, act then not later.

Credit sale

As hire purchase has declined in popularity, so the use of the credit sale has increased. This is now the most common way of buying household goods on credit. The difference between this and hire purchase is that the goods become the property of the buyer as soon as the deal is done. If you fail to make regular payments, whether the deal is interest free or not, rather than seizing back the goods, the lender will have to sue you through the courts for the money you owe.

Mail order

Originally confined to catalogues offering clothes and household goods, mail order is now used by many companies as a way of allowing consumers to shop at home for a huge variety of goods. However, if you send a cheque or authorise a payment through your credit or debit card when ordering goods, say from a charity catalogue, this is not a credit deal because you have paid before receiving your purchases.

It is a credit deal if you arrange to pay in instalments, whether or not interest is to be charged.

Many mail order companies operate through agents, who may be responsible for collecting regular payments from their customers who have chosen goods in the catalogue.

If you decide to become a mail order agent, always check whether or not you are liable for your customers' debts. As long as they, as individuals, are officially registered as the purchasers, and you keep detailed records, you should be safe, but always read the terms and conditions supplied to you by the mail order company before you begin 'trading'.

Being a mail order agent usually brings the benefits of commission. For every £1 your customers pay, you will receive cash or, more commonly, purchasing power from your catalogue to an agreed commission value.

Mail order can be an efficient way of spreading the cost of clothes and consumer goods, but it is always worth checking the catalogue prices against those for the same goods in the shops. If you find High Street prices are cheaper, you should ask yourself if you need the goods immediately or if you have time to save up for them.

The Banking Code

The Banking Code covers the responsibilities of banks and building societies and what consumers can expect in connection with:

■ Information about accounts, changes affecting accounts and choosing products and services.

■ How accounts operate, cards, PINs (personal identification numbers) and any lending and foreign exchange transactions.

■ Protection of personal information, accounts, cheque books, cards, electronic purses, PINs and passwords

■ What can be done if you find yourself in financial difficulties or you wish to complain to your bank or building society or to the independent Banking or Building Society Ombudsmen.

■ The Code sets the minimum standards of service that consumers can expect from all banks and building societies which subscribe to the Code.

The Code's 11 key commitments state that banks and building societies will:

1. Act fairly and reasonably.

2. Ensure that all services and products comply with the Code even if they have their own terms and conditions.

3. Give you information on services and products in plain language and offer help if there is any aspect which you do not understand.

4. Help you to choose a service or product to fit your needs.

5. Help you to understand the financial implications of

   ■ a mortgage

   ■ other borrowing

- savings and investment products
- card products

6. Help you to understand how your accounts work.

7. Have safe, secure and reliable banking and payment systems.

8. Ensure that the procedures staff follow reflect these commitments.

9. Correct errors and handle complaints speedily.

10. Consider cases of financial difficulty and mortgage arrears sympathetically and positively.

11. Ensure that all services and products comply with relevant laws and regulations.

The Consumer Credit Act 1974

The Consumer Credit Act was set up to establish, for the protection of consumers, a system administered by the Director General of Fair Trading, of licensing and controlling traders concerned with the provision of credit, or the supply of goods on hire or hire purchase, and their transactions.

The Act defines credit and hire purchase, it sets out how credit grantors must be licensed, how they may conduct their business and what protections and rights exist for consumers in relation to the advertising, marketing, setting up, administering and cancelling of credit or hire agreements. It also regulates the fast track access of consumers to information held by a credit reference agency.

The matters which the Act covers or explains include:

- Consumer credit and hire agreements (regulated agreements up to £25,000; small agreements up to £50).

- The meaning of credit.

- Restricted-use credit and unrestricted-use credit.

- Debtor-creditor-supplier agreements.

A copy of the Act can be obtained from:

Her Majesty's Stationery Office
Publications Centre
PO Box 276
London SW8 5DT

Tel: 0171 873 9090
Fax: 0171 873 0011

Chapter 4

Finance houses and money lenders

Highlight

Never accept credit from someone, no matter how respectable they seem nor how desperate you are, who is not registered as a credit grantor.

Some retailers now have their own financial services departments which manage the operation of all their credit products, primarily credit cards for use in their own shops but sometimes also offering personal loans as well. But behind many forms of credit you will find a finance house, which is running the card operation on behalf of a store.

You may also be introduced to a finance house when you want to buy a car, for example, on credit. Car dealers may have an arrangement with one particular finance house or they may approach several on your behalf in order to find you a good deal – and in order for you to be able to buy the car they are trying to sell.

Finance houses and money lenders also operate on a smaller scale and offer a more personal service, for example they may agree to visit you at home to collect instalments on a loan and you might be able to make weekly, rather than monthly, repayments.

These lenders are perfectly legal, and should not be confused with illegal money lenders. Always beware of anyone who calls at your home without an appointment offering any kind of credit, whether it be a loan or goods 'on tick'.

Check that the company you are thinking of doing business with belongs to a trade association, such as the Finance and Leasing Association (FLA), whose members range from small lenders to large banks, or the Consumer Credit Association (CCA), whose members specialise in Home Credit and who will grant you smaller loans sometimes without the need for you to have a bank account (see Appendix for details).

Home Credit companies often rely on the representative's personal relationship with the borrower, rather than on computerised scoring techniques, and serve those people who, because of low or irregular incomes, might otherwise find it difficult to get credit.

Never accept credit from someone, no matter how respectable they seem nor how desperate you are, who is not registered as a credit grantor. You could end up in a whole lot of trouble. And these loan sharks may try to force you to take out another loan to repay the first. At first they'll be friendly and helpful, but they'll almost certainly turn out be the very opposite, threatening violence or demanding your benefit book, for example. This is illegal and if it happens to you or someone you know, you must tell the police.

Paying up early

If you want to settle a loan or a hire purchase deal before it has run its course, you may be eligible for an early settlement rebate. Check before taking out a loan if this would be the case. It will depend on the sort of agreement you have signed. Even if you settle up early, you may well owe more than you originally borrowed. But if you can afford it, it might still be cheaper to pay the loan off in one lump sum than keep up repayments for the length of the agreement.

Plastic money

The term credit card is used to describe any plastic card with which you can obtain goods or services on credit. A card lets you pay for almost anything these days, from High Street fashion, a meal in a restaurant, a complete holiday or a train ticket. You can even get a cash advance by using them in an Automatic Telling Machine (ATM). To do this you will need a Personal Identification Number (PIN) which will be sent to you separately if you request it by the card issuer.

If using your card in person, the magnetic tape, or the computer chip which looks like a hologram, is electronically scanned and eventually your purchase or cash will be registered to your account with the card company. If you use your card over the phone or the Internet, the card number is noted and the card company notified of your purchase.

Usually a card is accepted without question, but if you are buying something expensive the shop assistant may well check with the card company that you really do have that amount of credit left. This they will do by phone.

Stores, restaurants, airports and the like are also regularly issued with lists of cards which have been lost or stolen. They ought to check your card against this list before processing your purchase.

You should always be very careful when using a card. Don't leave receipts which show your card number lying around on shop counters or in public rubbish bins. Ask the assistant for the carbon copy as well as the top copy. Keep the top copy to check against your statement. Destroy the carbon copy at home.

Only quote your card number on the phone to a company you know to be reputable. If you must use your card to buy through the Internet, find out first that the 'site' is secure.

- Never reveal your PIN to anyone. Memorise it – don't write it down anywhere.

- Sign your new card as soon as you receive it.

- Cut up old cards before you throw them away.

- Don't keep your cards with your cheque book.

- Keep your cards with you, not in a jacket hung up or on the back of a chair in public places, nor in a bag that you may put down, nor in a hotel room.

- Keep a tally of what purchases you put on your card, as you spend. Small amounts can add up very quickly to a large sum which can take you unawares at the end of the month when your statement arrives.

- Always try to pay off the total at the end of the month. If you can't, then try to pay more than the minimum amount. If you don't you could be paying out for a considerable time and if your card has a high interest rate this could prove an expensive way to buy.

- Keep your credit limit to something you know you can afford. If the card company says you can have more, you don't have to accept – say 'no' if you think a higher limit would tempt you to spend more than you should.

There are three main types of card:

Credit cards

The best known credit card names are Visa and Mastercard. Their systems are used by all the major banks and you can have more than one card and use the services through a variety of banks, whether or not you are a current account customer.

You will be given a personal credit limit on each card and once that limit is reached the card will be rejected by the computer system if you try to use it.

Repayments are made monthly and you will be given the choice of paying off the total amount you have spent, a 'minimum amount' – usually 5% of the total or £5, whichever is the higher – or any sum you can afford.

If you pay off the total balance shown on your monthly statement you will not be charged any interest. And if you manage your cards sensibly, you can effectively have a month or more interest free credit. So if you are really sure that you will be in a position to pay back everything you have spent each month then a credit card can be an efficient way

---

Highlight

And if you manage your cards sensibly, you can effectively have a month or more interest free credit.

---

of paying a month's shopping bills in one go – and at the same time having a record of what you have spent and where.

If you pay the minimum amount, interest will be added to the amount which is left and will form part of the balance on the next statement. Sooner or later, though, the full amount will have to be paid.

Some credit cards involve an annual fee, others don't. Some lenders waive the annual fee for the first year or so but then introduce it after you've been a customer for a while.

Some offer attractive 'perks' – for example Airmiles, or points which you can collect and which convert to cash or vouchers for goods. Others pay commission to a charity or an organisation, rather than the credit card holder, for every £1 you spend. Oxfam and the Labour Party are just two of the organisations which you can support by using their credit cards.

The annual percentage rate (APR) varies from lender to lender and represents the rate of interest you will pay on any money you leave unpaid on your credit card account after a month. Some companies offer an APR as low as 6%, some have rates which go well above 20%.

The personal finance pages of all major newspapers often publish details of how different APRs affect your monthly repayments. And the credit card companies themselves produce brochures and leaflets, usually designed to show that theirs is the best deal. Companies also use these statistics to persuade you to move the balance on another card, to theirs, and show how much you would save by doing this.

The following is an example of this. The table shows what you would pay, at various APRs, in interest over six months if your card balance stayed for that length of time at £500, £1000, £2,000 or £3,0000.

Outstanding balance	£500	£1,000	£2,000	£3,000
Interest at 29.0% APR	£65	£129	£258	£387
Interest at 22.9% APR	£50	£99	£198	£297
Interest at 22.7% APR	£49	£97	£194	£292
Interest at 9.9% APR	£24	£47	£95	£142
Savings over six months comparing the highest with the lowest	£41	£82	£163	£245

Some companies attract custom by offering a low APR for a limited time, but then raise the interest rate when that introductory period comes to an end.

If you really are reckoning on paying off the balance each month, the

APR is irrelevant, but remember that it is always a temptation to spend on a card when you can't afford it. So a low APR is worth searching for, especially if that card has no annual fee attached or offers the type of bonus points you want.

Your bills with shops, restaurants and other suppliers who have accepted your credit card are paid by the lender, who charges the shop a handling fee. Although it therefore costs companies to accept payment by credit card, they are prepared to pay as so many consumers these days expect to be able to shop in this way and will go elsewhere if they cannot. The cost is, however, ultimately reflected in the price that we pay for goods.

Chargecards

Highlight

Chargecards differ from credit cards in that there is no credit limit, but the amount spent must be paid off in full each month.

Chargecards differ from credit cards in that there is no credit limit, but the amount spent must be paid off in full each month. And if you have a chargecard you pay an annual membership fee to the card company.

Retailers' credit cards

Many shops, or groups of stores and petrol stations, now have their own cards. Customers can use them in the named shops only, but apart from that they operate in the same way as credit cards. You will be given a personal credit limit and can pay off a minimum amount, the total or a sum in between. You will pay interest, calculated on the APR agreed, on any outstanding amount.

Some companies which issue their own cards will not accept other credit cards in their shops.

Shop budget account

Some stores approach credit from a different angle. Rather than deciding the limit on your card before issuing it, you decide yourself how much you can afford to repay each month and this sets your limit. For example if you want to repay at £5 per month this will mean you can immediately spend up to around £100. Although the company will still do a credit check to make sure they agree with you.

If opting for this sort of card, it is better to decide what you want to buy first, rather than being tempted to spend on things you don't really need simply because you are able to. Interest is charged on the amount you owe, usually each month, at rates which vary from store to store, but your payments remain at the specified amount each month.

Credit unions

Credit unions are run by groups of people, who often know each other, and are based in communities – either a village or an area of a town, or in a workplace. A credit union is a legal organisation, run by its members, who agree to deposit money – usually just as much as they can afford and usually small sums – and use the credit union as a savings 'bank'.

The money accumulated from these savings is then available to members as small loans. Interest is usually charged at a very low rate, often around 1% a month. Loans can be repaid early without penalty.

Credit unions are popular in communities where people might not otherwise have easy access to credit, for example because of low or irregular incomes, and where only small loans are required. Workplace credit unions are convenient for people who might find it difficult to visit a more traditional lender or apply for a loan through other means. Credit unions often help members to budget, to save and to become familiar with the use of credit.

Changing your mind

So you've signed on the dotted line and agreed to a credit agreement. You may be buying goods on credit, opening a credit or charge card account, or taking out a mortgage. And then you change your mind.

Whatever the reason for your change of heart, and as long as you signed very recently, you may have rights which allow you to cancel. But there are exceptions.

- As a rule of thumb, if you signed the papers on the business premises of the company extending credit, or supplying the goods, you probably cannot cancel. If you take the papers home to think about the deal and sign them there, then you have probably turned what would have been an uncancellable agreement, into a cancellable one. Agreements do vary, though, so check the small print.

- If you agree to a credit deal on the phone, and the agreement is not subject to you signing papers, then the deal is probably uncancellable. Again, check your agreement.

- If you change your mind before the lender has signed the agreement, you have the right to say you don't want to go ahead with the deal.

Before you sign, look to see if the documents tell you anything about cancellation. If they don't, then ask. Ask, too, if you're setting up a deal on the phone. And if you are about to enter into an uncancellable agreement then think twice before signing or agreeing to anything.

If the agreement is cancellable, the time in which you are allowed to change your mind is referred to as a 'cooling off period' and it is usually five days. When you first sign you should be given a copy of the agreement, which should explain your cancellation rights. At this point the agreement is not in force and is 'unexecuted'. You should then be sent a second copy of the agreement through the post and this will again explain the cancellation rights. Your 'cooling off period' begins five days from the day you receive this second copy.

If you cancel an agreement involving goods which you have already received, then they have to be returned. Although it is officially the supplier's responsibility to collect them, if it is possible it is always better to take them back yourself and ask for a signed receipt. That way there can be no confusion.

If you must wait for the goods to be collected, then make sure they are kept somewhere safe where they will not be spoiled in any way. And if you can, regularly remind the company concerned that the goods are available and you are awaiting their collection. Always check that the company is not treating this as a 'defaulted' account. And never ignore letters from the company. Your credit reference could be at stake.

Pay up or else ...

If you get into difficulty and cannot repay a loan, lenders have a right to get back what you owe them. But it's illegal for them, or anyone acting for them such as a debt collector or a bailiff, to threaten you, either by phone, letter or in person. And they must neither use violence nor harass you at home nor where you work. The steps taken by a creditor to recover a debt always have, by law, to be 'reasonable'.

Debt is not a criminal matter. The lender or agent can go only to the county court for a judgment against you and this court does not deal with criminal proceedings. If you are being harassed, tell the police or the Trading Standards Department attached to your local council.

Highlight

If the agreement is cancellable, the time in which you are allowed to change your mind is referred to as a 'cooling off period' and it is usually five days.

No guarantee

Think very carefully before agreeing to guarantee any form of credit for another person. It might be a close relative, or even your best friend, but you may have to say 'no'. You are not providing a reference, you are actually guaranteeing that the loan will be paid. And if it isn't, then you will be liable for it. You might even be asked to be a guarantor and find your home is the security. If your friend or relative can't pay, and you can't pay, you could lose your home.

The middle man

Many people use a broker to find them the best financial deal, and this can include a loan or a mortgage. Brokers used to be found in offices, but now their premises – like those of the banks and building societies – are more like shops and can be found in any high street.

If you use a broker for insurance, his or her commission will be paid by the company you decide to take a policy with, but if you use a broker to find you a loan, you are likely to be charged for the service.

College days

Students traditionally have to learn to manage on very little money. But the days when a local authority grant would just about cover expenses, and a part-time job paid for extras, are long gone.

These days, the local authority grant – which is being phased out anyway – is unlikely to pay even for your accommodation. So unless you have the time and energy left after studying to do a well-paid part-time job, you are likely to need some sort of loan.

And soon you'll have no choice as you will be expected to repay the cost of your tuition as soon as you have left college and found a full-time job with a reasonable salary.

This is already the situation with the government student loan, which most students now apply for with help, if necessary, from their Students' Union or Student Services departments. If you are in full-time education you may be eligible for this student loan. Your college will know where you stand, how much you can borrow and should be able to give you an application form. You usually have to repay such a loan within about five years of leaving college, but if you are on a low wage – around the £1,000 a month mark – than you can ask to delay repayments. But don't forget that interest will mount up all the while you still owe any amount on the loan after you've left college.

Some students find they need extra cash or decide to plump for a loan from a bank or building society. Most of the major lenders offer interest-free loans especially designed for students. They are interest free while you're at college, but you may find varying rates of interest are introduced if you fail to repay within a certain time and once you're in a better financial position.

Highlight

Always try to act before the worst happens. Most lenders will listen sympathetically if they can see you are being sensible.

When trouble knocks at the door

The golden rule when faced with the prospect of money troubles is ACT NOW. Financial difficulties won't go away and if you do nothing they will certainly get much, much worse.

If you think you are going to find it difficult to pay one or several instalments on any accounts, whether it be the mortgage, a credit card or even a small amount owing to a mail order company – let the lender know immediately.

Always try to act before the worst happens. Most lenders will listen sympathetically if they can see you are being sensible. And the most sensible thing to do is to contact them. They may agree to freeze repayments for a month while you sort matters out or, if you need longer to get out of difficulty, they may agree to a lower monthly figure. If they do this, find out exactly how they will now classify your account. You want to avoid spoiling your credit history if you possibly can.

The quicker you accept that there is a problem to sort out, the better. These things will not go away if you ignore them. The longer you avoid action the more you risk interest building up at an alarming rate. You might also lose any goods you've bought on credit and if your home is secured against a loan or a mortgage, you risk losing that too.

You might be taken to court if you don't communicate with the companies you owe money to and you will probably find it difficult to get any credit in the near future if you fail to protect your credit history.

You may think that going into arrears on one or two small debts won't matter – well it will. It is never too late to sort out your money problems, so even if you are deeper in debt than you should be, and have ignored matters for a while, still do something.

Take action

■ Get together all the relevant paperwork – everything that details how much you owe, who you owe it to and how much you have agreed to pay.

■ Calculate how much money you have coming in and what expenditure is essential. The mortgage or rent, gas, water and electricity are all things that you should keep paying for, no matter what.

■ Prioritise any other credit agreements. For example, if you need the car to get to work, or to look for a new job, that might be an essential, too.

■ Work out how much money, if any, you have left over after the essentials are paid for.

■ Work out how much you can afford to pay to each lender. Be realistic. It is better to pay off a little, even if it's just a few pounds a month, than agree to a higher figure and get into difficulties again.

■ Contact all the lenders and explain your situation. They will all have departments used to dealing with this sort of problem. If you are not getting very far, ask to speak to a supervisor or a manager. Don't give up.

■ If the lender offers to freeze any interest you're paying, be grateful. They don't have to do this but it is always worth asking. If they agree it means anything you repay will come off the amount you borrowed.

■ Follow any telephone conversation with a letter, quoting the reference number of your agreement with that company. Send a copy of your financial statement – showing your income and outgoings – and list what you think you've agreed to pay and how and when. This way there can be no confusion and both you and the company will have written documentation confirming the conversation.

Help is at hand

If your debts are few and the lenders you contact are amenable to your offers, you may find you can handle matters yourself. But if you are in any doubt about what to do, or what you have agreed to – seek help.

Many Citizens Advice Bureaux employ specialist money advisers. Your local council may have a money advice unit. Or you may have a local Consumer Credit Counselling Service (CCCS). Your local library will probably have a list of the help available. Or look in Yellow Pages or Thompson's under Money Advice.

Never be embarrassed at revealing the whole mess to a money adviser. They will have seen worse! They will help you work out a budget and decide where you can cut down on spending. They will help you contact your creditors and make offers to pay reduced instalments. They are experienced in how to go about all of this and may even be prepared to speak for you and explain your situation in the county court if a lender decides to sue you for what you owe them.

Wolves in sheep's clothing

Make absolutely sure you go for assistance to a reputable money advice unit and not a back-street lender disguised as someone who wants to help. Go to an organisation you've heard of before, such as the CAB or CCCS.

Some cowboy outfits masquerade as money advisers, or credit repair companies (see the section on credit repair), but they are sometimes little more than loan sharks. They will lend to you when you are in difficulty, persuading you to pay off all your debts with one large loan from them. And in theory this sort of 'consolidation' loan might actually be a good idea – but not at the rates of interest you will be asked to pay.

If it looks like a deal you're being offered or that you see advertised in the paper is too good to be true – it probably is!

Going to court need not be a disaster

If you are really unable to pay your debts, your creditors – the people you owe money to – may well decide to take you to court. But this need not be a disaster. Although having a County Court Judgment (in Scotland called a 'Decree') may well affect your ability to get credit in the immediate future (depending on how quickly you settle and the amount you owe), having a court make a decision can help you sort out your money muddles.

Similarly, if a company sues you without justification, you will be able to explain why you feel you should not pay. If you have a justifiable case, a county court will decide in your favour. So if you receive a summons – in Scotland this will probably be called a 'writ' – don't ignore it and don't panic.

Fill in the forms which will come with the summons and send them back immediately. Get help to do this if you need it. Again, any bona fide money adviser will know what to do.

The forms give you a chance to state your case and to explain if you do not agree with what the plaintiff – in Scotland called the pursuer – is claiming. You must state realistically how much you can afford to pay each month to clear the debt and why. Your income and outgoings will be taken into account, as will any arrangements you have made to pay off other debts.

Highlight

If it looks like a deal you're being offered or that you see advertised in the paper is too good to be true – it probably is!

You may find that everything can be sorted out without you having to go to court in person. If you ignore a summons and fail to send back the forms, the county court will probably hear the case in your absence anyway and may then order you to repay the debt in one go or in repayments which you cannot afford. The court could also order that any goods involved be repossessed.

For a County Court Judgment made in your absence to be legally binding on you, you must have received a summons. But if you later tell a court that you haven't received one, when you have, you are breaking the law and could be guilty of perjury.

Don't worry if you do have to go to court. If you'd rather not go alone, or you want someone to state your case for you, find someone who understands your situation and who is good at explaining. This could be a friend, a relative, a solicitor or a money adviser. Take all your papers and documents with you so that you can prove that your figures are correct.

If you're being sued for £3,000 or less, the court hearing will be a relatively informal affair and will be held in private. The only people involved will be you and your representative if you have one, the individual or representative of the company claiming you owe them money and the District Judge or Court Officer – in Scotland this will be the Sheriff or Sheriff's Clerk.

The judge does not wear a wig and will try to make sure you are not intimidated by the hearing. He or she will want to make a decision with which both sides agree as quickly as possible, so you'll help your cause by being as co-operative and as efficient as possible. But don't be afraid to say if you don't understand something, or if you are not sure of your facts.

If the judge or officer decides you must pay, and how, a court order will be drawn up stating the amount you owe and how you should pay it. The benefit to you is that any interest will be frozen, so everything you pay will go towards getting rid of the debt and no extras will mount up while you're paying. But you must keep up the payments, which is why it is important to offer a realistic amount, or you can be taken back to court.

A record of the County Court Judgment will go on the public record and you might find it difficult to get credit in the near future. You should also be aware that if you apply for a financially sensitive job in the near future your prospective employer might ask your permission to check whether or not you have any County Court Judgments against you.

Chapter

Credit reference agencies

The role of a credit reference agency is to make it possible for lenders to quickly make accurate and responsible lending decisions. Credit referencing also helps lenders guard against fraud, which is a growing and serious problem. The cost of fraud is inevitably passed on to the consumer in the form of higher interest rates and higher prices, so it benefits every law-abiding citizen if fraud is prevented.

When you apply for credit, whether it be in person in a shop or at a bank, by filling in a form and sending it through the post, or on the phone, you will be asked to agree to a credit check being carried out. If you are not notified, or if the application form does not explain that this will be done, or if you refuse to give your permission, then the search cannot legally be carried out. If you do refuse, the chances are that your application will not go any further – in other words it won't be accepted, because most lenders insist on this as a condition of the credit application processing system.

Are you likely to repay?

If you agree to the credit check you are giving the lender permission to look at the information held about you by a credit reference agency. There is nothing sinister about this. It is very straightforward. All the information does is helps the lender decide whether or not you are likely to repay a loan, or pay for goods you are buying on credit, or honour an agreement to pay for the hire of equipment, like a television or a mobile phone.

This credit reference agency information helps lenders decide quickly – sometimes instantly as in the case of applying for credit in a shop – whether you are a good 'credit risk'. In most cases we are able to get instant credit thanks to the credit reference agency. It is certainly not a blacklist and people call it this only because they don't understand how the system works.

The businesses which use credit reference agencies include banks, building societies, finance houses and other loan grantors, shops, mobile phone and airtime suppliers and rental companies who provide goods for hire such as televisions and videos or kitchen and other electrical equipment.

Highlight

Credit reference agency information helps lenders decide quickly – sometimes instantly as in the case of applying for credit in a shop – whether you are a good 'credit risk'.

Not the whole story

The information about you supplied by a credit reference agency is often not the only information a lender has. They will also know the details that you have put on an application form or told them over the phone.

The credit reference agency has limited information. It does not know, for example, how much you earn, whether or not you own your own home, or what spare cash you have each month – you will tell the lender this and this information is not given to the credit reference agency. It remains confidential between you and the lender. If this detailed information is needed by the lender, it will be taken into account, along with the basic information from the credit reference agency, when the lender makes a decision.

A credit reference agency has financial and financially related information only. It knows nothing about your state of health, for example, or anything about any criminal convictions. It provides factual information only and leaves it up to the lender to make a decision. It does not tell the lender what it thinks of the information it provides.

There are two consumer credit reference agencies in Britain. The largest is Experian, the other is Equifax. They are necessarily very similar in the way they operate because they both have to abide by the strict laws which govern their business. And they both adhere to the rules which the credit industry has itself put in place to regulate the way credit information is shared.

What is credit reference information?

The information provided by the credit reference agency comes from several sources but falls into two categories – public information and credit account information.

Public information

The public information consists of:

- The UK Electoral Roll, obtained from local authorities. The Electoral Roll consists of information supplied to local councils by people themselves who fill in the forms distributed to households each October. New registers are published each February.

   Lenders use this information to help them confirm names and addresses. If you are not on the Electoral Roll, for any reason, it does not necessarily mean you will not get credit, but it does mean the lender will want some other proof of your address.

Always fill in the form from your local council very carefully – although you do not have to vote, it is illegal not to register. Make sure you include the exact names of adults and do not include any children unless they are soon to become 18.

■ County Court Judgments and Scottish Decrees issued in the last six years. These are supplied by Registry Trust, which is the official organisation which holds a list of judgments on behalf of the Lord Chancellor's Department.

■ Bankruptcies and Individual Voluntary Arrangements which are obtained from the London, Edinburgh and Belfast *Gazettes*. (see below).

Private individuals can declare themselves bankrupt, but more commonly bankruptcy applies to businesses and therefore company directors. A Voluntary Arrangement can be simply explained as a scaled-down versions of bankruptcy but which allows you some measure of personal control. In both cases you will be 'insolvent' – in other words the sum of your debts is more than the sum of all your assets. In Scotland, bankruptcy is called sequestration and Voluntary Arrangements are Protected Trust Deeds.

In the case of bankruptcy, your creditors, the people to whom you owe money, can take you to county court where your bankruptcy will be officially declared and an official will be appointed to take over your assets. He will negotiate with your creditors and arrange for your assets to be sold. You are legally allowed to retain certain assets, for example the essential tools of your trade, your bed and other necessary household effects. But your home and other assets are likely to be sold to pay off some or a proportion of your debts. Once the agreed reduced amount is paid, your debts will be cleared.

As a bankrupt you cannot become a company director or practice in certain professions, for example as a solicitor or an accountant. Bankruptcy ends once the order is discharged – in other words when all debts have been settled – or after three years. The exceptions are if you have been bankrupt in the previous 15 years or the court decides you have failed to fulfil your obligations under the bankruptcy legislation.

A Voluntary Arrangement can be used if you are definitely insolvent to stave off full-blown bankruptcy and can give you a breathing space in which to negotiate yourself with your creditors without the appointment of an official to take everything out of your hands, although someone will supervise the arrangement. Typically you would go to the county court and offer to pay your creditors a proportion of your debt,

Highlight

A Voluntary Arrangement can be simply explained as a scaled-down version of bankruptcy but which allows you some measure of personal control..

perhaps 50p in the £1. All your creditors have to agree before the court sanctions the arrangement. You would be responsible for selling off any assets necessary. Arrangements are officially completed once all the agreed sums have been paid.

Bankruptcies and Voluntary Arrangements are officially and publicly recorded in special publications called *'Gazettes'*. Discharges and completions are also listed in the *Gazettes*. This public information from the *Gazettes* is what appears on your credit file.

Credit account information

There is no such thing as a credit blacklist. In fact, probably the most important information held by a credit reference agency is that which shows how we are all conducting our credit arrangements. Most people in Britain are managing the credit that they have perfectly well. And this is what the credit reference agency information shows – which is why it is far from being a blacklist.

The UK's major lending companies have agreed to share with each other basic details of their customers' credit agreements. This lets them check, when someone applies for credit, how that person has repaid other lenders in the recent past or is repaying any current credit commitments.

In order for lenders to see each other's information, they store copies of their customer credit records with the credit reference agency. The credit reference agency acts as a go-between in the sharing process but does not own the information. It is owned by the lenders who store it with the credit reference agency. And they update the credit reference agency's database monthly.

The information will show what type of credit you have, what is your credit limit or the total amount borrowed, when you made the deal and how much you still owe.

It also shows that you are keeping to the agreements and paying off your loans or your credit card balances regularly and according to contract. If you are behind with payments, it will show that too and if you have defaulted on an agreement – in other words the debt has been recalled by the lender because they no longer feel you will keep to the contract to repay in instalments, this will be noted.

There is no need to worry if you have simply forgotten one month's payment and then have caught up the next month. Although we ought to pay everything on time, most of us miss one month at some time or another. It is only when you are seriously in arrears, or when you regularly fail to pay or don't manage to catch up with payments that you should be concerned.

Lenders can only see this credit account information if they belong to the credit reference agency's 'closed user group' – which is rather like a club. Lenders who use Experian belong to a closed user group called CAIS – Credit Account Information Sharing. Equifax's scheme is called Insight.

These groups are strictly regulated under a contract between the lender and the credit reference agency. Participating lenders can access credit account information only if they provide similar information to be shared.

Most lenders provide full details showing exactly how their customers are repaying their loans, for example, or keeping up to date on their credit cards. These lenders can see full details when they do a credit check. A few lenders send information to the credit reference agency only when a customer is seriously in arrears. So when they do a credit check, they will only see whether or not the customer they are 'searching' has similar problems. But these lenders are in the minority; more and more of them are now providing full details.

Lenders sharing information in this way must abide by the strict rules that clearly define the purpose for which the information may be used.

Searches which leave 'footprints'

When a lender wants to process an application for credit they 'search' the credit reference agency database for information about the customer at the address he or she has given and at any recent previous addresses. They can search addresses up to six years old.

This search is conducted much in the same way as a word or phrase is found by a word processor or a personal computer. But the credit reference agency's computer will only search for a name with an address. Lenders cannot search for a name only nor for an address only – the system just won't allow it.

Each time a search is made, it leaves a 'footprint', detailing which company has accessed the credit reference agency database and when. This allows you, the consumer, to see who has sought information about you, although you should know already because you will have given your permission for the search to be made, by signing the consent clause on the credit application form – which you should always read – or by agreeing orally to the search if the application was made by telephone.

This record of searches forms part of the information seen by lenders, although they do not see who has accessed the information. In other words they do not know which company has searched for information about you. Nor do they know what the result of that search was.

Lenders need to see this record of searches because it allows them to identify 'abnormal activity' – a large number of applications for credit made by the same person in a short space of time – which could signify fraud or over commitment by a consumer.

For example, if you start at one end of the high street, and apply for credit in every available shop, by the time you reach the far end, stores will know that you appear to be on a bit of a spree. They will not necessarily refuse your applications, but they are unlikely to grant you credit there and then, because what you have done is not normal activity. They might wonder whether you are either trying to get as much credit as you can for suspicious reasons, or if you are taking on more credit than you can handle. If this was the case, and they granted you even more credit, then they would be acting irresponsibly and perhaps be encouraging you to get into debt.

Shopping around

Shopping around for the best credit deal should not create this sort of abnormal number of searches because a search should only be conducted when you actually apply for credit. Simply asking what deals are on offer does not constitute an application and you should make it clear, if you're making an enquiry only, that you are not applying for credit.

When shopping around, people usually obtain basic details of offers from a range of lenders and probably make an application only in response to the one which they consider the best deal.

If you are using a middle man, a car dealer perhaps, or a mortgage broker, make it quite clear to them that by asking for various quotes you are not agreeing to several searches. Only when you find the quote you like will you go ahead with an actual application for credit.

Searches stay on the credit reference agency database for 12 months.

You should always know that a search 'footprint' is going to appear on your file, because you should always be informed by the lender, orally or in writing, if a credit reference check is being carried out. They must, by law, tell you this, just as they should notify you that information about your credit account with them is to be stored with a credit reference agency and that they will do credit search as part of your 'account management', in the prevention of fraud and for debt tracing.

Always read any credit application form carefully before you sign and you will see where it explains about credit referencing. If you don't understand any of it, or you can't see where you are giving permission for a search, ask.

Similarly you should always listen carefully when arranging credit over the phone, and don't be afraid to ask the person on the other end of the line to go over things again if you haven't understood. This 'consent' is very important and is your legal right as a consumer.

Repossessions

The Council of Mortgage Lenders (CML) provides the credit reference agency with details of those people whose homes have been repossessed. Only mortgage grantors who belong to the CML and who provide information themselves can see these details.

Fraud prevention

The Credit Industry Fraud Avoidance System (CIFAS) contributes to the credit reference agency's database to allow lenders to guard against granting fraudulent credit applications. This shared information also protects the innocent victims of fraud, for example people who might have had their credit cards stolen. Only lenders who belong to the scheme can provide or receive this information.

If you report your credit card lost or stolen this will be marked on the file. In this way, if the thief then tries to use your card, perhaps by showing it as identification in order to get more credit in your name, anyone doing a credit search will know that this might not be the real you. If it is you – perhaps you've found your card or have had a replacement issued – then you will be able to prove your identity. The thief who is trying to impersonate you won't find this so easy to do.

If this happens to you, and you are asked for proof of who you are, don't be offended. Instead be glad that people are making it difficult for a fraudster to steal your identity.

The Gone Away Information Network (GAIN) helps lenders share information when a customer who owes them money has tried to avoid paying their debt by moving without letting anyone know.

Factual information only

The credit reference agency supplies only entirely factual information and it does not make lending decisions. It has no details about nor

Highlight

The Gone Away Information Network (GAIN) helps lenders share information when a customer who owes them money has tried to avoid paying their debt by moving without letting anyone know.

knowledge of your race, religion, sexual preference, political persuasion, employment details, medical history, council tax or criminal records. It doesn't show how much money you have in your current bank or building society account either and has no record of your savings, nor of any stocks or shares or other assets you own.

Different lenders employ different lending policies and attach varying degrees of importance to the details supplied by the credit reference agency, and those they gather from the customer, depending on the amount of risk they wish to take when deciding whether or not to grant credit. Using the same information, one lender may say 'yes' where another will say 'no' (see the section on Credit Scoring on page 71).

The credit reference agency is not told how the information it provides has affected a lender's decision, nor whether an application for credit has been granted or declined.

Your right to see the information held about you

The Consumer Credit Act 1974 and the Data Protection Act 1998 give people the right to see, for £2, a copy of the information held about them by a credit reference agency which any lender could see when doing a search on them. If you apply for this it is called your credit 'file' (see Chapter 6 for more details).

Experian publicises this fact and runs a consumer education programme aimed at making sure people know they have this right. As a result they send information to nearly 750,000 people every year.

All you have to do is send your name and address, and a list of your addresses over the past six years, with a cheque or postal order for £2, to the credit reference agency address at the end of this book. An example letter to a credit reference agency is provided on page 51.

By law the credit reference agency must send you the information within seven working days of receiving your request. If you want to query any of the information, the credit reference agency must let you know what they are doing about your query within 28 days of receiving it.

Credit reference information is not normally sent by the credit reference agency to anyone other than the person it concerns at the address listed in the credit reference agency's records as their current home. Once you have received your file, you can contact the credit reference agency to resolve any queries or for general advice.

Example letter to credit reference agency requesting copy of file

Claire Smith
34 Anywhere Street
Anywhere
Anyshire
AA0 0AA

(01234) 567890

11 April 1999

ABC Credit Reference Agency
Creditown CC2 0CC

Dear Sir/Madam

Please send me a copy of my credit reference file. I enclose a cheque (or postal order) for the statutory amount of £2.

The above address is my current address. In the past six years I have also lived at and

78 Nowhere Street
Nowhere
Nowhereshire
BB0 0BB

I look forward to receiving my file within seven days of you receiving this request.

Yours faithfully

Claire Smith

Claire Smith

If you want to know more

When you get a copy of your file you will also receive a leaflet which explains what all the different information means and your rights in relation to that information. How to read your file is dealt with in Chapter 6. But if you want it explained in more detail, or you have difficulty in reading the leaflet, you can contact the credit reference agency and they will help you. Or you can take your file to a money adviser who will do the same.

Lenders' decisions

If you send off for a copy of your file because you have been refused credit, and after receiving the information still do not understand why, you have to go back to the lender and ask. The credit reference agency does not make lending decisions and it cannot tell you why your application for credit has been refused, or accepted – because it does not know, only the lender knows that.

If you get your file and do not understand, or disagree with, some of the information which has been put there by a lender, you should contact that lender, as only they can sort this out for you.

The credit reference agency will help, however, and if necessary will put you in touch with a named individual at the organisation which provided the information, so that the query can be sorted out at source. If necessary, the credit reference agency will contact a lender on your behalf, but it is usually better to do it yourself, or to get a money adviser to help, as you know the facts better than anyone and will probably have any paperwork that can prove your argument if there is one. An example letter is provided on page 54.

Association and disassociation

When you get a copy of your file you may be surprised to see that it includes information about people you live with or have lived with and who have the same surname as you. In official language you are 'associated' with them.

Experian says the most common query they receive concerns the fact that people with the same surname at the same address are linked on the credit reference agency database. These 'associations' exist for a reason. Lenders sometimes take a family household's finances into account when making credit decisions because they want to make sure that a family does not take on more commitments than it can afford.

Highlight

After a 'disassociation' has been created, when any credit reference check is carried out, the lender sees only details about you and anyone with whom you have a financial link.

Lenders are allowed to do this by law because their experience shows that the finances of individual members of a family sharing a home do have an effect on each other.

However, if you really do not want to be linked to members of your family, and if you have no joint finances with them, then these links can be easily broken. All you have to do is ask the credit reference agency to create what is called a 'disassociation'. You need to ask for a separate 'disassociation' from each person concerned. For example, if you live with or have recently lived with a parent and a brother and a sister, and have no joint financial arrangements with any of them, then ask to be 'disassociated' from your parent and also from your brother and also from your sister. Ideally they should sign the letter too, but if that is not possible it doesn't matter. An example letter requesting disassociation is provided on page 56.

After a 'disassociation' has been created, when any credit reference check is carried out, the lender sees only details about you and anyone with whom you have a financial link.

And if you again apply for a copy of your file, you will see that the details of the other people will no longer be there.

'Disassociation' is fairly simple for the consumer. It only becomes complicated if you share a first name or an initial, as well as a surname, with a family member. Sometimes fathers and sons, or mothers and daughters, have the same first name or initial. If this is the case, the credit reference agency will help by putting a note on the file alerting lenders to this, telling them that a 'disassociation' exists and that they must check they are using only the correct details when making a credit decision.

Letter to lender requesting amendment of credit reference file

Claire Smith
34 Anywhere Street
Anywhere
Anyshire
AA0 0AA

(01234) 567890

11 April 1999

XYZ Lender
Lenderville LL0 0LL

Dear Sirs

I have obtained a copy of my credit file from the ABC credit reference agency and disagree with the information supplied by you concerning A/C No 123456.

I enclose a copy of the relevant section of my file and copies of correspondence with your company showing that this information is incorrect.

Please amend your records and correct the information held by the ABC credit reference agency and any other relevant credit reference agencies.

Please contact me at the above address or telephone number if there is anything you need to discuss with me or if my request causes any problem.

Please confirm in writing to me that these amendments have been completed. Thank you.

Yours faithfully

Claire Smith

Claire Smith

You cannot 'disassociate' from people with whom you do have financial connections, for example a joint loan or mortgage or a joint credit card – lenders really do need to know about them as well, because their finances affect yours. Maintenance payments from an ex-partner do not count as a financial connection.

When a 'disassociation' is created by the credit reference agency, it notifies the other credit reference agency, which saves you having to go to the bother of doing it yourself. It also tells any lenders who have searched the credit reference agency's database for information about you in the past six months. So if you were refused credit because of a family member's poor credit history, you can ask for your application to be reconsidered.

Consumers do not need to 'disassociate' from people with whom they simply share a house or flat – unless they do, coincidentally, have the same surname. You are not linked to people, even if you live with them, who have a different surname as you, unless you have some form of joint finances.

In the same way, you do not need to 'disassociate' from people who have moved into somewhere you used to live, or who lived at your address before you, unless they have the same surname as you, which is very rare.

You might hear, or read, that you can be refused credit because the person who lived in your house or flat before you had financial problems. This is not true.

County Court Judgments

If you pay off the full amount of a County Court Judgment (CCJ) or Scottish Decree within 28 days, it is no longer recorded by the credit reference agency or on the public record. So the golden rule is always pay judgments in full immediately if you can and check that the record has been deleted.

Unfortunately, most people incur judgments because they can't afford to pay the debt, and so they do get recorded. And they then stay on the record for six years from the date of judgment. But even if you have paid nothing off your debt, the judgment will disappear after six years.

If a judgment has been paid, however, it can be marked as 'satisfied' on the credit reference agency database. To get this done you need to contact the county court concerned. This will be shown on your file and the credit reference agency will give you an address and phone number if you need them to.

Letter of disassociation to credit reference agency

Claire Smith
34 Anywhere Street
Anywhere
Anyshire
AA0 0AA

(01234) 567890

11 April 1999

ABC Credit Reference Agency
Creditown CC2 0CC

Dear Fiona Lawson

Re: File No: 1223456789

Thank you for your letter of 23 April 1999 with which you enclosed a copy of my file.

I note that my file contains information about Mr Joe Smith, my brother, Mrs Gladys Smith, my mother, and Mr William Smith, my father. Although I have lived at the same address as these members of my family, I have no financial connections with them. Would you therefore please create disassociations between myself and them.

Please send me a copy of my file once it is amended so that I may see that the disassociations have been created. Thank you.

Yours sincerely

Claire Smith

Claire Smith

You have to pay the County Court £3 and it will issue you with a Certificate of Satisfaction – in Scotland you have to contact the 'Pursuer' (i.e. Plaintiff) for a 'Proof of Payment'. Once the certificate has been issued , the public record with the Registry Trust, and subsequently the credit reference agency's database, will be updated. If you need your file updated urgently, then send the original certificate, not a copy, to the credit reference agency and they will amend their records. An example letter to a credit reference agency requesting an update to a recorded County Court Judgement is provided on page 58.

Notice of Correction

A Notice of Correction is a statement of up to 200 words in which people can explain or expand upon the information held about them. It is not often used to 'correct' information, because if information is wrong the credit reference agency will alter it. A Notice is more commonly used to explain why the information is as it is; an example is provided on page 60.

For example, you may have defaulted on a credit agreement or incurred a County Court Judgment or Scottish Decree because of a sudden change in circumstances – perhaps you have been made redundant, or your partner has been seriously ill or died. The information held by the credit reference agency which shows this default, or the judgment, is therefore factually correct and cannot be altered as it is a true account of your credit history. In this situation, the credit reference agency would advise you to use a Notice to explain the special circumstances which led to your financial difficulty and, if you want, they will help you to word the Notice.

The credit reference agency must add the Notice to its database within five days of receiving it and will send it to every lender who has searched you in the last six months. If the Notice concerns a County Court Judgment or Scottish Decree, it will be sent by the Registry Trust to both credit reference agencies.

Once you have a Notice on your file, any lender who searches the credit reference agency about you in the future will see it. And they must read it and take it into account when deciding whether or not to grant you credit. It does not mean you will automatically get credit, but it does mean that your special circumstances will be explained and the lender will know why you got into difficulty.

Example letter to credit reference agency re County Court Judgment

Claire Smith
34 Anywhere Street
Anywhere
Anyshire
AA0 0AA

(01234) 567890r

27 April 1999

ABC Credit Reference Agency
Creditville CC2 0CC

Dear Fiona Lawson

Re: File No 123456789

Thank you for your letter of 23 April 1999 with which you enclosed a copy of my file.

I am writing to ask you to update the entry concerning County Court Judgment No: 987654321 issued by Smalltown County Court in the sum of £500 on 29 September1998. I enclose the original Certificate of Satisfaction from the County Court and ask that you amend the record to show this CCJ as satisfied.

Please send me a copy of the amended file. Thank you.

Yours sincerely

Claire Smith

Claire Smith

Highlight

If you want to add a particular Notice and the credit reference agency decides it is inappropriate, they will tell you why and will refer your notice to the Office of Fair Trading. Or you can contact the Office of Fair Trading yourself.

The credit reference agency will not accept Notices which are libellous, obscene or frivolous. If you want to add a particular Notice and the credit reference agency decides it is inappropriate, they will tell you why and will refer your notice to the Office of Fair Trading. Or you can contact the Office of Fair Trading yourself. This government department will then make a decision as to whether or not your Notice should be added to your file. The Director General will give you the opportunity to comment and the whole matter should be resolved within two months of the Director General receiving information from you and the agency.

If the agency does not reply within 28 days of receiving your Notice of Correction or replies that it will not accept your Notice of Correction, you also have the right to ask the Director General of Fair Trading to look into the matter. The address is:

> The Director General
> Office of Fair Trading
> Field House
> 15–25 Bream's Buildings
> London
> EC4 1PR

Your letter should give the following details:

i)   say that you are writing pursuant to section 159(5) of the Consumer Credit Act 1974;

ii)   give your name and address and that of the agency;

iii)   give details of the entry you wish to have corrected saying why it is wrong and why you will be disadvantaged if it is not changed;

iv)   give the date when you sent your Notice of Correction to the agency;

v)   include copies of any correspondence between you and the agency and a copy of your Notice of Correction.

An example letter is provided on page 61.

Example letter to credit reference agency with notice of Correction

Claire Smith
34 Anywhere Street
Anywhere
Anyshire
AA0 0AA

(01234) 567890

27 April 1999

ABC Credit Reference Agency
Creditown CC2 0CC

Dear Fiona Lawson

Re: File No 123456789

Thank you for your letter of 23 April 1999 with which you enclosed a copy of my file. The information you hold is factually correct, but I would like to explain the relevant circumstances and ask you to add the following Notice of Correction to my file.

Notice of Correction

I, Ms Claire Smith, of 34 Anywhere St, Anywhere, Anyshire, AA0 0AA, wish to notify anyone searching my file that the financial difficulties reflected by the County Court Judgment and the defaulted account details supplied by XYZ Lenders were caused by my being made redundant on 29 March 1997 was out of work for some time, but have been in full-time employment since 1 January 1998 The defaulted account has now been settled and the CCJ has been paid. I no longer have any outstanding debts and would ask anyone searching my file to take this into account when considering an application by me for credit.

Please send me a copy of my file once the Notice has been added. Thank you.

Yours sincerely

Claire Smith

Claire Smith

Example letter to Office of Fair Trading

Claire Smith
34 Anywhere Street
Anywhere
Anyshire
AA0 0AA

(01234) 567890

3 May 1999

The Director General
The Office of Fair Trading
Field House
15-25 Bream's Buildings
London EC4A 1PR

Dear Sir/Madam

I write to ask you to arbitrate in the case of my dispute with ABC Credit Reference Agency pursuant to Section 159(5) of the Consumer Credit Act 1974. I enclose all relevant correspondence from which you will see that ABC credit reference agency is refusing to add to my file the Notice of Correction which I supplied to them.

Please contact me if I can provide you with any further information.

Yours faithfully

Claire Smith

Claire Smith

Amendments

Most of the information held by both credit reference agencies in Britain is accurate. But mistakes do occur. If you find a mistake on your file, don't panic and don't get unnecessarily angry. Simply contact the credit reference agency, providing all the proof you have such as statements or letters, and they will correct the information.

It is not in the interest of the credit reference agency, nor in the interests of lenders, for any information to be inaccurate. And so credit reference agencies actually advise consumers to check their files regularly.

They do have to follow certain procedures, however, to make sure that you are right and to make sure that any mistake is corrected everywhere it is held.

For example, if you find a mistake in the details of one of your credit accounts on file, a correction has to be authorised by the lender concerned. This is because that lender owns the information, not the credit reference agency. And also because the lender needs to correct its own records to guard against the error being repeated when updates the credit reference agency's database.

If an error concerns public information, and the matter can't be sorted out easily, the credit reference agency will liaise with the public body concerned to put the matter right, perhaps the local authority if it is a mistake in the Electoral Roll.

Accuracy of information is of extreme importance to lenders, consumers and credit reference agencies. As previously explained, the information held by the credit reference agency is, in the main, a copy of information held elsewhere – by local authorities, other official bodies and by lenders. Experian explains that while its credit reference agency is dependent on lenders and other organisations to provide correct information, it accepts it has a duty to take all measures possible to ensure that the data it stores is accurate.

Credit repair companies

Credit repair companies claim to be able to remove or alter information held by credit reference agencies and charge considerable amounts for this 'service'. It is generally agreed that the claims made by credit repair companies are bogus. These companies sometimes masquerade as advisers when they are actually looking for a way to lend you more money at high interest rates. Or they may simply charge you for advice that you can get elsewhere for free.

Highlight

Never be tempted to
claim that you have not
received a summons
when you have. If you lie
to a court you are
committing perjury – and
that is a criminal offence.

Credit reference agencies work with bona fide money advisers, such as the National Association of Citizens Advice Bureaux, the Consumer Credit Counselling Service and Money Advice Trust, as well as local Trading Standards Officers and the Office of Fair Trading, the Lord Chancellor's Department, solicitors and the Office of the Data Protection Registrar, to ensure that people do not pay unnecessary fees to companies which claim they can 'repair' credit information.

Credit repair companies claim to be able to rid people of County Court Judgments or Scottish Decrees. As explained elsewhere, these stay on record for six years from the date of judgment and can only be cancelled if the sum is paid within a month of judgment or if a person genuinely has not received the relevant summons. In this case, if you do owe the money, but have not received the summons, you must consider whether or not the summons is likely to be re-served. If it is, then the whole process will begin again and, unless you can now afford to pay the debt immediately, the length of time a County Court Judgment is recorded will be prolonged. In other words, the judgment that you dispute because you didn't receive the summons will disappear, but if you are then taken to court again, a new one will appear. Obviously, if the disputed judgment was a few years old, the situation has worsened. You have stopped the first six-year clock ticking, but started a new one.

Never be tempted to claim that you have not received a summons when you have. If you lie to a court you are probably committing perjury – and that is a criminal offence.

People with debt problems or questions about their credit reference information should always contact a bona fide money adviser or the credit reference agency, for example Experian's Consumer Help Service, which employs more than 100 people to give consumers free advice and to help consumers put right any genuine errors. The only payment is likely to be the statutory £2 for a copy of the information held by the credit reference agency. You do not have to part with any larger sum to a credit repair company.

When you should check the information held about you

Divorce or separation

If you have been married, or lived as a couple with someone for any length of time, you are likely to have had joint financial commitments, perhaps a joint mortgage or other loan, a joint bank account or a joint credit card.

When you part company it is important to make sure that these ties are broken. This does not happen automatically, even if you are legally divorced. If you do nothing you could find that within the next six years, when you apply for credit, your ex-partner's credit history will be taken into account. If he or she has a poor history, you could be affected by it. You might find that members of his or her family, or even his or her new partner, are linked to you, because they may have the same surname you have or had, or because they live where you used to.

So as soon as you separate, check what joint finances you have and arrange with the lenders or anyone else involved to change the agreements. This may not always be straightforward. One of you might have to sign over the mortgage to the other, for example. Or you might have to pay off one loan and take out another. You may find you owe each other money.

Even if it gets complicated, it is worth doing. Lenders are quite used to this situation. They will help you sort matters out. It is often in their interest to make sure that loans are not forgotten and that everyone involved knows who is liable for what. If you are consulting a solicitor, he or she will help if necessary – but don't pay for legal advice unless you need or want to, when all you have to do is contact the various lenders.

Once all financial ties have been broken, write to the credit reference agency for a copy of your file. Then ask for the 'disassociation' to be created as described earlier.

Moving home

Moving can be an expensive business. And it is typically a time when people take on several new credit arrangements. There is the mortgage, if you're buying a home, for a start. Then you may want to pay for new carpets on credit, or arrange to rent a television and video. You might need to buy new kitchen equipment... the list goes on and on.

It is always advisable to get a copy of your credit reference file before you begin shopping for these big items. That way you can identify if there will be any problems before they occur, and sort them out first, if possible.

It is also advisable to work out what credit you are going to need. Add up the cost of all the things you want to buy. It might be easier – and cheaper – to get one loan to cover everything rather than taking on several separate credit arrangements. This way you will also avoid the possibility of lots of credit searches appearing on your credit reference file in a short time. (See the section on 'footprints' on your file.)

If you do find yourself turned down for credit and you think the only reason can be the number of searches on file, don't lose your cool and don't try to explain to a sales assistant who might not understand as much about the system as you do. Simply find out the address of the store's credit department and write, explaining that you are moving house and have had to make lots of separate credit purchases, and ask them to reconsider your application.

If you're not on the Electoral Roll

It can sometimes take more than a year after you have lived somewhere for you to appear on a credit reference agency's copy of the Electoral Roll. For example, if you move house in November, and therefore miss the local council's form, and also fail to tell the council that you have moved in, then you will have to wait until the following October, when the next forms are distributed, to register.

It takes the council several months to compile the annual register and it takes about two more months for this information to be entered on to the credit reference agency's database.

It's always good idea to inform your local authority as soon as you move. You may be in time to get on to the register even though you've missed the official form. Do it at the same time you sort out your council tax.

If you are refused credit because you are not on the Electoral Roll – mobile phone companies can be particularly strict about this, for example – explain the situation and offer further proof of your address, a utility bill or a credit card statement will usually be accepted. If the store cannot reverse the decision, write to the company's head office.

Moving your accounts

When you move home, always move your credit accounts with you. Get a copy of your credit reference file to check that you have identified them all – that way you won't forget mail order or other accounts which you may not have used for a while.

Your monthly credit card statements will have a form on them which you can fill in to notify the lender of any changes, including change of name or address. But you may not be getting regular reminders if a loan is paid by direct debit, for example, or if an account is dormant. The payments may be up to date, but your address on the lender's records won't be.

It's up to you to remember to let all the lenders and official bodies you deal with know that you have moved. When writing include your name, your old address, your account number and your new address.

Highlight

If you are refused credit because you are not on the Electoral Roll – mobile phone companies can be particularly strict about this, for example – explain the situation and offer further proof of your address.

In the excitement of moving you can easily forget to make that month's repayment, particularly if you don't get a reminder. And if your statement goes to your old address, you may not remember to make next month's either. Don't let arrears mount up in this way. Let everyone know your new address immediately you move.

If you do this, even if you are not on the Electoral Roll but all your credit accounts have moved to your new address, a lender will be able to see that you really do live where you say you do.

Getting married

When a couple get married, the woman often changes her name. But this does not mean she loses her maiden name. All her credit accounts in her old name will still be shown on her credit reference file. If she lets the lenders concerned know her new name, they will note this as an 'alias' on the credit reference agency's database.

When you get married, let all the lenders you have dealings with know your new name at the same time that you notify the official bodies, like the tax people and insurance companies if you have any policies or pensions.

Be aware that if you change your name, you will automatically become linked to those people you live with who share your surname, so if you move in with your new in-laws, their recent credit histories can affect your ability to get credit. (See the section on 'disassociation'.) Even if you don't move in with them, your husband may have lived with them in the past six years, so a link between you and them may be created through him.

Leaving home

When you leave home, it is usually because you have decided you want to be independent to some degree from your parents or other family members. But for credit reference purposes, this independence is limited.

If you apply for credit, the lender will ask you for your previous addresses, sometimes up to six years, and they will then see the recent credit histories of those people you lived with who have the same surname as you.

You may be tempted to prove your independence by getting the credit reference agency to create 'disassociations' from the members of your family. But be warned. If they have good credit histories, in other words they pay their credit deals on time and have no County Court Judgments, the fact that they are linked to you might help, especially if you are young and are applying for credit for the first time.

When you ask for your first loan, or apply for your first credit card, the lender will do a credit reference check. If you have no other credit accounts, they will not be able to see that you know how to handle credit. The fact that your family does handle their credit sensibly, might tip the balance in your favour.

Bereavement or serious illness

If a partner, a relative or a close friend dies, the last thing on our minds is sorting out the finances. Similarly, if someone close to us is taken seriously ill, we are more likely to be concerned with visiting them in hospital than making sure the bills are paid.

However, when someone dies, it can save a lot of sorting out later on if you at least make sure that anyone to whom payments should be made is notified of the situation. You can always write a short note and explain that you will be in touch later to find out what else needs doing.

Lenders have sometimes been accused of callous behaviour, when they have chased debts left by people who have died. And this can cause anguish for a bereaved family. But unless someone tells them, lenders won't know what the situation is. They will be sympathetic right from the start if they understand what has happened and they will help you finalise matters when you are ready.

When someone is seriously ill, they may not be in a position to make, or even remember, the repayments on a loan, for example. You will be doing them a huge favour if you take this task on and make sure they avoid the shock of finding they are in arrears once they get better.

The trouble is, of course, that we often do not know what bills are paid regularly or how. We may not even realise that we might be jointly liable for a debt or that joint financial arrangements mean that our partner's or a family member's inability to pay through death or illness can affect us further down the line.

If you are too upset to cope with such matters when someone close to you dies, ask a trusted friend to do it for you. People really want to be of help at a time like this and you will always find someone only too happy to feel that they are being of use.

All of us would like to be well organised, but the day to day business of work and homelife often gets in the way. It is when tragedy strikes that the real value of record keeping is revealed.

So don't let your own death or illness cause even more grief for your family and friends. Make a list of what commitments you have, who they are with, how much needs to be paid and when. And keep it up to date. In this way, if you are taken into hospital, or you die, someone can

Highlight

Don't let your own death or illness cause even more grief for your family and friends.
Make a list of what commitments you have, who they are with, how much needs to be paid and when.

quickly and easily sort things out for you and make sure that the lenders involved know what the situation is.

Strict controls on who can see a credit reference file

Access to credit account information held by the credit reference agency is strictly limited.

It can be accessed only by lenders who are members of a 'closed user' information sharing group. They must be credit grantors and must be registered with the Office of the Data Protection Commissioner under the Data Protection Act 1998 and be licensed by the Office of Fair Trading under the Consumer Credit Act 1974.

Companies which access public information only – in other words who don't see credit account information but do see the Electoral Roll, County Court Judgments and Bankruptcies, are subject to less stringent controls, as the information is publicly available from other sources.

If you are unhappy about the information held about you by a credit reference agency, or by anyone who holds personal details about you, you can complain to the Office of the Data Protection Commissioner (see Appendix). If you feel you have been unfairly treated over a credit deal involving £25,000 or less, you can complain to the Office of Fair Trading. It is simpler to try to sort matters out in the ways described in this book first. But if you are still not satisfied, the official regulator will investigate your complaint.

If you're turned down for credit

If you're turned down for credit, don't panic – and don't get angry, especially not if you are in a store and the only person to shout at is a shop assistant. The chances are that you will know more, from reading this Guide, than they do about how credit works. And it is unlikely that they will be senior enough to alter a credit decision made by their computer.

Even if you deal with the manager, he or she will probably not have the authorisation to change a credit decision which has been made according to the rules laid down by their head office.

By making a fuss you are drawing attention to yourself. Being refused credit anywhere can be annoying, but if it happens in public it can be embarrassing, too. Don't make matters worse. Show that you are well informed and in command by asking the right questions and maintaining your dignity.

You may sometimes be told that you have been refused by a credit reference agency. This is never true, but shop assistants, particularly if they are undertrained, new, or part time, do not always know how their own systems work. They do not understand that the decision to say 'no', while perhaps based on credit reference information, is always based on their employer's lending policies. And it is difficult to tell a customer that you do not want their business. It is easier to blame someone else.

If you are turned down for credit, the organisation concerned should give you some idea why. They must also tell you if it was because of information contained in your credit file and, if so, the name and address of the credit reference agency they used.

If this is not offered, ask for it. If the person dealing with you cannot tell you, ask for the address and telephone number of their credit department or head office. A letter requesting details of a credit reference agency constructed by a letter is shown on page 70.

In a bank or building society, you will probably be dealing with someone who is quite well informed. They may be able to tell you there and then the main reason for the refusal. They will certainly be able to tell you whether or not it was based on credit reference information and, if so, the address to write to for your file. If for some reason they cannot tell you this, they will be able to refer you to someone who can.

If you have to contact a head office or credit department, ask to be told the principle reason for refusal. The 'principle reason' may not be easy to identify (see section on Credit Scoring), but if it is you should be told. And remember that you have the right to ask a lender to reconsider your application, although it is sensible to sort out any problems first, or the answer is likely to be 'no' again.

Finding out why

Lenders are understandably wary of telling people too much. They don't want to reveal the details of how they make lending decisions because it could help a criminal put together a fraudulent application, for example by answering the questions on an application form differently – in other words lying about his circumstances in such a way that the lender gave him credit he shouldn't have, or simply that they didn't wish to give him.

Example letter to lender requesting details of credit reference agency used

Claire Smith
34 Anywhere Street
Anywhere
Anyshire
AA0 0AA

(01234) 567890

11 April 1999

XYZ Lender
Lenderville LL0 0LL

Dear Sir/Madam

Re: Loan application No 0000000000

Thank you for letting me know that my recent application for credit has been refused. If information provided by a credit reference agency was relevant to this refusal, please let me know the name and address of the agency used and provide me with any form you might have which will enable me to apply for a copy of my file.

If your rejection of my application for credit was based on information other than that provided by a credit reference agency please let me know the principle reason for your refusal. Thank you.

I look forward to hearing from you as soon as possible.

Yours faithfully

Claire Smith

Claire Smith

No right to credit

Nobody has a right to credit. There are some simple rules about being refused. By law, you cannot be refused credit simply because of where you live. Nor can you be refused because of the colour of your skin, your sexual preference or your religion. And lenders do not take these things into consideration. But they can decide not to give you a loan, or let you have goods on credit, because of how much you earn, or how long you've lived in your current home, or because you don't have a phone. This is their right. Just as you can refuse to lend a friend £10, so can a lender refuse to give you £1,000.

Having said that, lenders make money from extending credit. They want to say 'yes'. If they said 'no' too often they'd go out of business. So most of them use what is considered to be the fairest way of making a decision – credit scoring. What they are really interested in is whether or not you are going to repay them.

Credit scoring

Credit scoring is really a very simple and obvious technique once it is explained.

When you apply for credit, each detail on your credit application is given a different score. The more questions on the form, the more sophisticated the scoring system is likely to be.

These scores are added up and the total is the rating for that application. Remember that applications are rated, not people.

Scoring is usually done by computer. It can, however, also be done manually. But using a computer is much, much quicker. And it means that personal bias plays no part in the decision reached. A computer cannot form an opinion about someone by looking at them, or by hearing their voice. It can base its decision only on the information fed to it. Scoring by computer is called automated scoring.

When setting up its own scoring system – building what is called a 'bespoke scorecard' – the lender will decide who it wants to lend to. Usually this will be anyone who is going to honour the agreement and repay the loan. A lending company will look at its existing customers and those whom it has done business with in the past, and work out who are the best and who are the worst at honouring their agreements.

Highlight

When setting up its own scoring system – building what is called a 'bespoke scorecard' – the lender will decide who it wants to lend to.

Let's pretend

Let's pretend that a bank lent £20,000 each to 100 people in the last five years, and of those 100 people only 10 failed to make regular repayments. (Of course, in real life, the sample would be much larger and the details much more complicated.) If it was trying to work out a scoring system, the bank would try to find out what those 10 had in common with each other but not with the 90 who did repay.

Say that none of the 10 had telephones at home, they all earned under £8,000 a year, they all drove cars and they all rented rather than owned their own homes.

Then, looking at the 90 good customers, we discover that they all earned over £20,000 a year, they were all aged over 25, they all had home telephones, they all drove cars and they all owned their own homes.

This is a gross simplification, of course, and a lender would have much, much more information than this, but these facts alone would tell the lender that whether or not you drove a car was unimportant, but that having a telephone and renting might be significant. How much you earn is obviously part of the equation. Being over 25 appears to be relevant.

Building a scorecard with only these details would be easy (but unwise, of course). An income of more than £20,000 would get a high score. An income of less than £8,000 would get a low score. Incomes in between would probably get varying scores. An age of under 25 would attract a low score. A home telephone would get a high score, lack of a phone would get a low one. Rented homes would get a higher score than a home that was owned.

Sometimes lenders have a few hard and fast rules. For example, they might decide that they just do not want to lend to people under 20, or people with a County Court Judgment (CCJ) in the past year. So no matter how your other details scored, you would simply be refused credit because you had a new CCJ or were only 19.

Using the example above, you can see that different people would achieve different scores. If you rented your home but had a phone, earned £7,900 but were 29 – then some of your details would get high scores and others would get low. It would be your total score which would decide whether or not you were granted the credit you'd applied for. If it was a low score, it might be difficult for the lender to identify the 'principal' reason for refusing you credit.

Most lenders' automated scoring systems are programmed to accept applications which score highly and reject those at the bottom, but most also have a grey area. If you are in the middle your application might well be referred. Which means that the decision is not cut and dried, but has to be given extra consideration.

There's no such thing as your credit rating

It is up to the lender to decide the profile of the people it wants to lend to, depending on how much risk it wants to take – and as long as it stays within the law. Lenders are not allowed to attribute a score to your ethnic origin, your gender, your religion or your sexual preference, for example.

Each lender may use a different scoring system. And each lender probably has different scorecards for each of its different 'products', depending on what customers they want to attract.

For example, the scorecard for bank loans of around £5,000 especially designed to attract young people as customers would be very different to the one for high interest mortgages aimed at people who needed to borrow more than £150,000.

So you can see that there is no way anyone has a 'credit rating' or a 'credit score'. Your 'score' will depend on which lender you apply to, what your circumstances are at the time and what you are applying for.

Lenders do not have to use their own, or bespoke, scorecards. They can use generic ones. These will have been worked out, in the way illustrated in the pretend example above, by specialists – mathematicians and statisticians – to suit certain businesses.

Support for credit scoring

The Office of Fair Trading supports the principles of credit scoring and recognises its important contribution to responsible credit granting. Its increased use over the past 15 or so years has proved that credit scoring is one of the most consistent, accurate and fair forms of credit assessment available.

Most lenders who use credit scoring have agreed to follow the recommendations laid down in the *Guide to Credit Scoring*, which was revised in 1993. The *Guide* is a document put together by lenders' trade and professional associations and by the credit reference agencies and lays down a few basic rules.

One of the *Guide's* recommendations is that customers should understand how credit scoring works, and this is something that has been welcomed by the Office of Fair Trading.

Highlight

The Office of Fair Trading supports the principles of credit scoring and recognises its important contribution to responsible credit granting.

Guide to Credit Scoring

The following are just a few extracts from the *Guide to Credit Scoring* which should help consumers know what to expect if they are refused credit:

The introduction states:

In drawing up the new Guide, the industry has recognised the Office of Fair Trading's concern that consumers should be given reasons for refusal of credit. It is important that reasons are meaningful and useful to consumers; there are also real dangers to lenders and their customers if credit scoring systems are opened up to manipulation and fraud.

This Guide is of value to all involved with the provision of consumer credit and is commended to both developers and users of credit scoring systems. We believe that it will also be of interest to consumers and to those concerned to protect the interests of consumers...

The organisations which have drawn up the Guide To Credit Scoring 1993 have agreed that their members who use credit scoring will be expected to observe its principles where they apply to their business.

Credit is not a right. The purpose of this Guide is to ensure that everyone can be confident that credit granting decisions based on credit scoring are made fairly.

The *Guide* says:

Principles of decision making

Credit scoring should not discriminate on the grounds of sex, race, religion or colour. All other available relevant factors, if legal, should be examined in the development process. A credit scoring system should be designed and used in a way that conforms with all relevant legislation. Particular attention should be paid to the following Acts of Parliament, or regulations made under these Acts by any bodies or Commissions given statutory power by these Acts:-

a) The Consumer Credit Act
b) The Sex Discrimination Act
c) The Race Relations Act
d) The Fair Trading Act
e) The Employment Protection Act
f) The Data Protection Act.

This list is not exhaustive.

Credit grantors may take factors other than the credit score into account when making a decision and are not obliged to rely solely on the credit score. These factors may include:-

a) verification of identity
b) validation of application details
c) applicants' income and existing commitments
d) credit reference agency information
e) the credit grantor's own prior experiences relevant to that application
f) any security offered.

Credit grantors will not refuse credit solely on the grounds of place or area of residence. The area of residence may be included in a credit scorecard when it is a properly weighted factor.

However, credit grantors do have the right to refuse credit in areas where they are not represented, or if they have reasonable grounds to believe that servicing that account would place the safety of their property, agents and/or employees at risk.

Cut-off scores may be established or changed by credit grantors at their discretion on the basis of overall financial considerations. Such changes should apply to the whole or a subset of the system and should not be used to discriminate against individual applicants.

When an application is not immediately acceptable but might be accepted on the basis of further information or investigation, it should be treated as a referral and not a refusal: for example, if identity cannot be established, the application form has not been completed fully or there have been a number of recent credit reference agency searches.

Where an automated system has been used and an application is 'referred', a manual underwriting process may be introduced. Where a manual system has been used, the application may be referred to another lending officer. In either case, further information may be sought from the applicant and/or a third party.

Information to consumers

Credit grantors are encouraged to tell applicants that credit scoring may be used as part of the decision-making process. If applicants ask whether credit scoring will be used they must be informed of that fact.

When credit grantors, in the normal course of business, write to applicants to tell them that their applications have been declined by a credit scoring system:

a) they will tell them that credit scoring has been used and, on request, provide a simple explanation of how it works;

b) without jeopardising the security or integrity of their scoring systems or running the risk of fraud, they should give as clear an explanation for the refusal as possible by providing the principal reason for the decline, such as:-

- a decline based on credit score
- a decline based on credit reference agency information
- a decline based on specific policies e.g:-
  over-commitment
  home ownership (for a secured loan)
  under age
  not employed
  existing account performance
  the credit grantor is not represented in the applicant's area.

If unsuccessful applicants who have not been given a written reason for refusal write to appeal, credit grantors should comply with these principles in their response. If reasons for refusal are given orally, staff should be appropriately trained.

Review of refusals

If a rejected applicant wants to appeal against a refusal of credit based on a scoring system, the applicant must be informed of the proper procedures to do so.

Credit grantors should reconsider the application if it is supported by relevant additional, verifiable information. Such a review should, if appropriate, be conducted by a different lending officer to the one originally handling the application. Credit grantors may grant credit on terms different from those originally proposed as the financial basis of the transaction.

Credit grantors should establish, within their own organisation, designated officers to whom appeals should be sent. They should have the authority to override the original decision and their addresses should be given to applicants who wish to lodge such an appeal.

Credit grantors should keep their appeals procedures under continual review.

Repeat applications

Any application for credit should be treated as a new application and assessed accordingly. An applicant for credit should not be rejected solely on the grounds of having made a previously rejected proposal or proposals to that credit grantor. Exceptions to this will be:-

- where it is apparent that the re-application has been completed dishonestly;

- where multiple applications are received with identical information during a period when there has been no change to the credit scoring system or the cut-off point.

Complaints

Credit.grantors should establish complaints procedures within their organisations and supply information about the procedures to customers who wish to make a complaint.

When a credit grantor is a member of an organisation which offers an independent complaints procedure relevant to the administration of credit scoring, customers should be told of this if their complaint cannot be resolved satisfactorily through the internal complaints procedures.

You can see from these extracts from the *Guide to Credit Scoring* that those lenders who follow the *Guide* are trying to give better customer service, and fairer treatment to consumers, than is sometimes thought. But they do have to keep one eye open for the fraudster, which is to the benefit of all of us.

Because lenders together are dealing with millions of applications for credit each year – around 70 million a year at the last count – mistakes are sometimes made. If it is a genuine error, the lender will want to put it right, especially if the customer is polite. You can still be firm, but try not to lose your temper, even if you are upset.

Consumers do have rights. In the UK and Europe consumers are thought to be particularly well served, not just by the law, but because there are many pressure groups campaigning on our behalf.

Our new UK Data Protection Act is based on a Directive from the European Union and similar legislation has been, is being, or very soon will be, introduced across the whole of the European Economic Area.

So know your rights, but remember that with rights come responsibilities.

The right of lenders to offer you credit, and to charge you interest on loans, brings with it the responsibility not to encourage people into debt, and not to make life too easy for the criminal.

Your right to be treated fairly when applying for credit brings with it the responsibility to borrow wisely.

Chapter

How to read your credit reference file

Refer to the example credit reference file beginning on page 84.

Electoral Roll information

This is a copy of the Electoral Roll, sometimes called the Voters' Roll or Electoral Register, held by your local council.

It gives the name of the local authority, then lists the address and addresses you have given when you asked for a copy of your file.

It shows the people who are or were registered to vote at that address or addresses, with dates when they registered and when they ceased to be registered there. This information can go back several years.

The dates showing when you were registered and when you ceased to be registered may not coincide exactly with when you actually moved in or out. What they show is when the local council recorded you as being there.

The fact that previous occupants are listed does not mean that you are linked in any way. The rest of the file, which is all the information a lender might see when carrying out a search in response to your application for credit, will confirm that people with the same surname at the same address only are linked.

The dates show when each individual was registered.

This information helps lenders confirm that the addresses given on application forms, as current or previous addresses, are correct.

You should contact the credit reference agency if:

■ Your name is spelled wrong.

■ The address details do not coincide exactly with the way you write your address (this may be something you'll eventually need to sort out with the local council or the Post Office).

■ You disagree with the dates.

■ You know you are registered (perhaps you have already voted or received a polling card) but your name does not appear.

Public record information

County Court Judgments

These are records of any money judgments made by the county court against you. If you have none, there will be no information in this section. This information is provided to the credit reference agency by Registry Trust, an independent organisation set up with the co-operation of the Lord Chancellor's Department. The Lord Chancellor is responsible for county courts.

Judgments stay on the record for six months from the date they were made, whether or not they have been paid in part or in full.

If you have a County Court Judgment the information will show your name and address, the date of judgment, the amount owed, whether or not the judgment has been Satisfied and the date of Satisfaction, the name of the court, the type of judgment, the source of the information, for example the Lord Chancellor's Department, and the case number.

You should contact the county court, quoting the case number, if:

- You need the name of the Plaintiff – the person or company which sued you (known as the Pursuer in Scotland). Credit reference agencies do not have this information.

- You did not know the judgment existed and did not receive a summons.

- You need a Certificate of Satisfaction to show you paid the judgment in full within one month. This costs £3. In this case it will be deleted from the credit reference agency's records.

- You need a Certificate of Satisfaction to show you have paid the judgment in full, but not within a month. This also costs £3. In this case it will still stay on the record for six years from the date of judgment, but will be marked as Satisfied.

  Scottish courts do not issue Certificates of Satisfaction. Instead, you need a letter confirming that you have paid the decree, and when, from the Pursuer.

You can contact the County Courts Customer Service Unit, Court Service, 6th Floor, South Side, 105 Victoria Street, London SW1E 6QT, or the credit reference agency, if you are unable to find out the address of the county court listed.

You should contact the Registry Trust at 173-175 Cleveland Street,

London W1P 5PE if you disagree with the details recorded about an English or Welsh judgment or a Scottish decree. The current search fee is £4.50.

Queries about Northern Irish judgments should be sent to The Enforcement Office, 7th Floor, Bedford House, 16/22 Bedford Street, Belfast BT2 7DS. You should send any documents this office gives you to the credit reference agency so it can update its records.

Bankruptcies and Voluntary Arrangements

This information is obtained by credit reference agencies from the official Gazettes and the Insolvency Service.

If you have not been bankrupt nor entered into a Voluntary Arrangement to pay off your debts, no information will appear on your file. If you have, the information will show the date of the bankruptcy or Voluntary Arrangement, the amount involved, the court name if relevant, the type of arrangement, whether or not a bankruptcy has been annulled or discharged, or a Voluntary Arrangement completed, and the source of the information, for example The Department of Trade and Industry.

If you have a query about a bankruptcy, you should contact the Official Receiver who originally dealt with your case.

Queries about Voluntary Arrangements should be made to the supervisor of the individual arrangement.

Credit reference agencies will amend their records if you send them documents proving that the information should be updated.

Bankruptcies and Voluntary Arrangements stay on the consumer credit reference agencies' records for six years.

Credit account information

Depending on the type of credit, each entry could show:

- Your name and address as it is held by that lender.
- The name of the lender.
- The date the account was opened.
- The date the account was settled or closed.
- The type of account, e.g. Mortgage, Budget Account, Loan or Credit Card.
- If the account has been defaulted and the date of default.

- If the default has been satisfied or paid in full.

- The monthly terms of the agreement.

- The current balance or amount you still owe.

- Your credit limit.

- Your status history for the past 12 months, shown as a series of figures, e.g. Status 000021100000. These show how you have kept to the contract and if you have not by how many months you are or were in arrears. In the case of a closed account these figures relate to the last 12 months the account was open.

- A summary of your payment history over the 36 months since the details were updated. In the case of a closed account this is the history of the account's final 36 months. These figures will show how many times in that 36 months the account was one or two months in arrears and how many times it was more than three months in arrears, e.g. 'No of status 1-2 is 3, No of status 3+ is 0'.

- The date the details were last updated by the lender.

- If there is a Notice of Correction attached to the file.

Other details might show that:

- The agreement was ended early and why.

- An individual has been reported as deceased.

- An individual has been reported 'gone away'.

- An account has been transferred to the dealer or retailer who introduced the customer to the lender.

- There is an Arrangement to Pay – the lender has agreed to vary the amount of the monthly repayment for a certain length of time.

- A Debt Management Programme exists – which will have been negotiated with the creditor on behalf of the consumer by a money adviser.

- An insurance claim has been made under a credit protection policy.

- The accuracy of an account is being queried by the consumer.

Because the credit account information belongs to the lenders and not the credit reference agency, if you have any queries or you disagree with the information you should contact the lender concerned by going back to the place where you obtained the credit.

If you have difficulty doing this, or you cannot resolve the problem this way, the credit reference agency should be able to give you the name of someone to talk to at that lender's office or, if necessary, by liaising with the lender on your behalf.

The lender will notify the credit reference agency if the information needs to be amended and you can then ask the credit reference agency for another copy of your file so that you can check that the information is now correct.

You may not always immediately recognise the name of the lender on an account. This may be because your store credit card is issued and managed by a finance company on behalf of the retailer, or because you did not realise who the lender was when you took out a personal loan through a car dealer, for example.

Associations and aliases

These will list people with whom you have joint financial arrangements and any previous names, for example a woman's maiden name, in which you have held an account.

Previous searches

These entries record each time the credit reference agency database has been searched for information about you in the past 12 months. No search record should be a surprise to you as a search can only be carried out with your consent and in response to an application by you for credit or when you have applied to open a new current account. Banks have to do a search in this situation as part of their process to guard against money laundering.

Each entry can include:

- Your name and address as provided by you to the lender you applied to.

- The name of the lender (this is shown only on a credit file when it is sent to a consumer; lenders do not see who has searched).

- The type of credit applied for and sometimes the amount involved.

- The date of birth you gave the lender.

■ The length of time you told the lender you had been at your present address.

■ The date of the search.

If you have any queries, if the information is incorrect, or if a lender appears to have searched more than once in relation to one application, you should contact the lender. Only if you cannot resolve the matter with the lender you should contact the credit reference agency.

Previous and forwarding addresses

This information lists any previous or forwarding addresses that you have had. When you request of copy of your file you should give any previous addresses of the past six years as the credit reference agency can only provide you with the information at the address or addresses you supply.

If you fail to reveal a previous address to a lender when asked, that lender will see that you do have a relevant previous address. Sometimes failing to give a previous address can be a genuine oversight, but it can also be the way in which a fraudster tries to hide a poor credit history in an attempt to obtain credit which he should not be granted.

Repossessions

This information, provided by a lender who is a member of the Council of Mortgage Lenders, will show if the individual's house has been repossessed or been voluntarily surrendered. It may include:

■ The address of the repossessed property.

■ The address from which the application for the mortgage on the property was made.

■ The address to which the customer has moved.

Credit Industry Fraud Avoidance System

This information appears on a file if a lender has reported that a fraud is known to have been committed, or if your card has been reported lost or stolen. It may list:

■ The name used.

■ The address used.

■ The date the information was recorded.

■ The name, address and phone number of the credit grantor

supplying the information.

■ The name of a contact at that company and the case number.

■ The type of fraud with the code letter to which it is referred under the scheme.

■ A warning that lenders seeing the CIFAS flag must not assume that the person applying for credit is connected to a fraud; if a lender sees this information when you apply for credit they will carry out further checks to determine that you are the innocent party. If there is a CIFAS flag on your file, contact the credit grantor's representative listed for more information.

Notice of Correction

If you have added a Notice to your file this will appear with the date it was added.

Notices can also be added by the credit reference agency, for example if there has been difficulty in creating a 'disassociation' between people with the same surname at an address due to their having the same first name, or if there is confusion about an address as it appears on the Electoral Roll.

Example credit reference file

```
                                    Consumer Help Service
                                    PO Box 8000
                                    Nottingham   NG1 5GX

Ms C Smith
34 Anywhere Street
Anywhere
Anyshire
AA0 0AA                             Date: 29/05/99
                                    Our reference:
123456789


                    YOUR CREDIT FILE

Enclosed is a copy of your credit file which contains all
the information we hold about you. We have included a
leaflet explaining the different types of information that
may be contained in your file and the steps you should
take if you have any queries.  PLEASE READ THIS LEAFLET
AS IT PROBABLY ANSWERS ANY QUERIES YOU MIGHT HAVE.

Most of the information we hold about you has been
provided by organisations with which you currently have a
financial relationship or those with which you have had a
financial relationship in the past. If you have any
queries about the information they have given to us, you
should contact them first so that they can authorise any
changes to our records.

Would you please include the reference number above in
any future correspondence with us.


                    ADDRESSES SEARCHED

34 Anywhere Street, Anywhere, Anyshire AA0 0AA
78 Nowhere Street, Nowhere, Nowhereshire BB0 0BB
```

(Continued on next page)

Example credit reference file (continued)

```
              ELECTORAL ROLL INFORMATION

The following names are confirmed on the electoral roll
from and until the dates shown at the addresses quoted:

Present Address

Local authority ANYWHERE
34 Anywhere Street, Anywhere, Anyshire AA0 0AA

Flat 2
SMITH CLAIRE              From 1996 to present

Flat 1
NEIGHBOUR JOHN            From 1995 to present


Previous address/es

Local Authority    NOWHERE
78 Nowhere Street, Nowhere, Nowhereshire BB0 0BB

SMITH CLAIRE                   From 1988 to 1996

SMITH JOE            From 1990 to 1997

SMITH WILLIAM                From 1982 to present

SMITH GLADYS            From 1982 to present


NOTICE OF CORRECTION

Reference A1B2C3D4 - See final page of file
```

Further information about the Electoral Roll is given on Page 77

(Continued on next page)

Example credit reference file (continued)

```
              OTHER PUBLIC RECORD INFORMATION


Claire Smith, 34 Anywhere Street, Anywhere, Anyshire AA0 0AA

Information type SATISFIED JUDGMENT,
Date 05/97 Amount £481, Satisfied 07/97

Court name SOUTHTOWN, Case number 12345678

Source LORD CHANCELLOR'S DEPARTMENT



Claire Smith, 34 Anywhere Street, Anywhere, Anyshire AA0 0AA

Information type JUDGMENT,
Date 04/94 Amount £369, Case number 87654321

Court name NORTHTOWN, Source LORD CHANCELLOR'S DEPARTMENT



Claire Smith, 34 Anywhere Street, Anywhere, Anyshire AA0 0AA

Information type BANKRUPTCY ORDER,
Date 01/94, Source LONDON GAZETTE



Claire Smith, 34 Anywhere Street, Anywhere, Anyshire AA0 0AA

Information type ORDER OF DISCHARGE,
Date 01/97, Source LONDON GAZETTE



Mr Joe Smith, 78 Nowhere Street, Nowhere, Nowhereshire BB0 0BB

Information type VOLUNTARY ARRANGEMENT,
Date 02/94, Source DEPARTMENT OF TRADE & INDUSTRY



Mr Joe Smith, 78 Nowhere Street, Nowhere, Nowhereshire BB0 0BB

Information type VOLUNTARY ARRANGEMENT COMPLETED,
Date 02/97, Source DEPARTMENT OF TRADE & INDUSTRY
```

Unless a County Court Judgment was paid within one calendar month, it will continue to be retained on file for six years from the date of the judgment. Please see page 78 for further information.

If you have paid a judgment you should contact the county court in question and request a Certificate of Satisfaction. Please see page 78 for further information.

If you have been annulled or discharged from bankruptcy provide the credit reference agency with documentation from the court or Official Receiver and the record will be amended. Further information about bankruptcies can be obtained on Page 79.

Bankruptcy details are kept on record for six years even if discharged or annulled.

Queries about Voluntary Arrangements should be taken up with the Supervisor of the Arrangement. If you have completed the arrangement and your file does not yet show this, send the credit reference agency a copy of confirmation from the Supervisor so that it can update its records.

This information shows that the conditions of the arrangement have been met. Details of the Voluntary Arrangement will continue to be held on your file for six years from the date of arrangement.

(Continued on next page)

Example credit reference file (continued)

```
                              LENDERS'   RECORDS
```

All queries about account
information should be sent to
the company shown. An
explanation of the status
history is provided on page
80. Settled accounts are kept
on file for six years from the
settlement date. The status
history in respect of a settled
account relates to the period
of time prior to the date of
settlement.

```
Ms Claire Smith, 34 Anywhere Street, Anywhere, Anyshire AA0 0AA

Date of birth 22/10/60
XYZ LENDERS BUDGET ACCOUNT
Started 19/04/98, Balance £344, Credit Limit £360
Status history 000000UU
In last 7 months, number of status 1-2 is 0; number of status 3+
is 0
Details updated 15/04/99
```

Account reflects that all payments have been made on time.

```
Ms Claire Smith, 34 Anywhere Street, Anywhere, Anyshire AA0 0AA

Date of birth 22/10/60
Arrangement from 01/97 to 08/97
CREDIT CARDS R US  PLC CREDIT CARD,
Started 19/06/96, Balance £1126,
Credit Limit £1300, Status history 000000U00000
In last 15 months, number of status 1-2 is 0; number of status
3+ is 0
Details updated 14/03/99
```

Account reflects that all payments have been made on time.

```
Ms Claire Smith, 34 Anywhere Street, Anywhere, Anyshire AA0 0AA

ZYX MOBILE COMMUNICATIONS RENTAL
Started 05/07/94, Default £348, Defaulted 06/07/97, Balance
SATISFIED
Status history 8
Details updated 19/04/99
```

*Defaulted accounts are kept on file for six years after the date
of default even though they may have been paid.*

```
Ms Claire Smith, 34 Anywhere Street, Anywhere, Anyshire AA0 0AA

Date of birth 22/10/60
LOANS LIMITED LOAN
Started 4/06/96 Balance £2107  Status history 000011UU0000
In last 15 months, number of status 1-2 is 2; number of status
3+ is 0
Details updated 14/03/99
```

*Account reflects that two payments have been made one month
late.*

(Continued on next page)

Example of credit reference file (continued)

Mr William Smith, 78 Nowhere Street, Nowhere, Nowhereshire BB0 0BB

GIVUMONEY FINANCE LIMITED BUDGET ACCOUNT
Started 16/05/97 Balance £344, Credit Limit £360, Settled 01/05/97
Status history 000U
In last 12 months, number of status 1-2 is 0; no of status 3+ is 0
Details updated 14/12/98

Settled accounts are kept on file for six years from the settlement date.

Mrs Gladys Smith, 78 Nowhere Street, Nowhere, Nowhereshire BB0 0BB

TALKALOT PHONES LIMITED RENTAL
Started 27/08/93 Default £348 Defaulted 15/10/94 Balance £1
Status history 8
Details updated 07/01/97

Defaulted accounts are kept on file for six years after the date of default.

WHO HAS SEARCHED YOUR FILE?

Ms Claire Smith, 34 Anywhere Street, Anywhere, Anyshire AA0 0AA

Searched on 15/07/98 Time at address 02 Years 03 months
Searched by XYZ LENDERS
Application type UNRECORDED ENQUIRY

Ms Claire Smith, 34 Anywhere Street, Anywhere, Anyshire, AA0 0AA

Searched on 15/05/98 Date of birth 22/10/60 Time at address 02 Years 03 months
Searched by CREDIT CARDS R US
Application type REVOLVING CREDIT

> The details shown below are those input by the company when they made the search. Details of companies who have searched are kept on file for 12 months. If you have any queries concerning the information, contact the company who has searched. This information does not imply that an account is held with the company. Further information about previous enquiries is on page 81.

(Continued on next page)

Example credit reference file (continued)

The credit reference agency has been told about Previous and Forwarding addresses by the lender shown below. If you have no connection with any address recorded under your name, contact the company concerned.

```
              PREVIOUS AND FORWARDING ADDRESSES

Ms Claire Smith     Moved from:  78 Nowhere Street, Nowhere,
                                 Nowhereshire BB0 0BB
                    to:          34 Anywhere Street,
Anywhere,
                                 Anyshire AA0 0AA
                    Source:      ZYX Mobile Communications
```

Details of any connections between members of your household/family are listed. If the connection no longer exists write to the credit reference agency asking for a disassociation.

```
              PEOPLE WITH JOINT FINANCES


Ms Claire Smith, 34 Anywhere Street, Anywhere, Anyshire, AA0 0AA

Associated with:    Mr Joe Smith
Association type:   Joint loan
Date:               25.12.91
Source:             Credit For You Ltd



              NOTICE OF CORRECTION

3007080/Credit

I, Ms Claire Smith, of 34 Anywhere Street, Anywhere,
Anyshire AA0 0AA, wish to notify anyone searching my file
that the financial difficulties reflected by the County
Court Judgment and the defaulted account details supplied
by XYZ Lenders were caused by my being made redundant on
29 March 1997. I was out of work for some time, but have
been in full-time employment since 1 January 1998. The
defaulted account has now been settled and the CCJ has
been paid. I no longer have any outstanding debts and
would ask anyone searching my file to take this into
account when considering an application by me for credit.

Added 10/04/99 PDQ
```

Appendix

Useful addresses

If you need help or advice or want to make a complaint, the following addresses may be useful.

Always first try to contact the local branch of the organisation you want to speak to, if one exists. The people there will refer you on if necessary.

Money advice free of charge

You will find the address and telephone number of your local **Citizens Advice Bureau (CAB)** in the Phone Book. A money advisor will help no matter now small or how large your problem and will help you contact your creditors. They may also be prepared to represent you in the County Court.

You local council's **Trading Standards** department – sometimes called Consumer Protection department – may run a money advice unit. Even if they don't, they might be able to help or tell you who to ask. Look in the Phone Book under your local council's name. In Northern Ireland look under the Department of Economic Development.

The Consumer Credit Counselling Service: 0345 697301 For advice over the phone or to make an appointment at the branch nearest your home. If appropriate a counsellor will speak to your creditors for you and arrange an agreed Debt Management Programme for you.

National Debt Line: 0121 359 8501
For help and advice with debt problems.

Radio One Line Freephone: 0800 110 100
For round-the-clock confidential advice on all cash matters.

National organisations

National Association of Citizens Advice Bureaux NACAB

Myddleton House
115-123 Pentonville Road
London N1 9LZ

Federation of Independent Advice Centres

4 Dean's Court
St Paul's Churchyard
London EC4V 5AA

The regulators

Office of Fair Trading, Consumer Information Line: 0345 224499

For guidance on where to get practical help with consumer problems.

Office of the Data Protection Commissioner, Enquiries: 01625 545745

For information on all apsects of data protection

Wycliffe House
Water Lane
Wilmslow
Cheshire SK9 5AF

County courts organisations

Registry Trust: 0171 380 0133

Holds a record of all County Court Judgments

173-175 Cleveland Street
London W1P 5PE

County Courts Customer Service Unit: 0171 210 2266

Court Service
6th Floor, South Side
105 Victoria Street
London SW1E 6QT

Trade associations

British Bankers' Association: 0171 216 8800

Pinners Hall, 105-108 Old Broad Street
London EC2N 1EX

Building Societies Association and Council of Mortgage Lenders: 0171 437 0655

3 Savile Row, London W1X 1AF

Finance and Leasing Association: 0171 836 6511

Imperial House. 22 Kingsway
London WC2B 6UN

British Retail Consortium: 0171 647 1500

5 Grafton Street
London W1X 3LB

Consumer Credit Trade Association: 0171 636 7564

Tennyson House
159-163 Great Portland Street
London W1N 5FD

Consumer Credit Association: 01244 312 044

Represents lenders who
specialise in Home Credit

Queens House, Queens Road
Chester CH1

The Ombudsmen

Ombudsmen are government-appointed independent arbitrators.

The Banking Ombudsman: 0171 404 9944

70 Grays Inn Road
London WC1X 8NB

The Building Society Ombudsman: 0171 931 0044

Millbank Tower, Millbank
London SW1P 4XS

Credit reference agencies

Experian Consumer Help Service: 0115 976 8747

PO Box 8000
Nottingham NG1 5GX

Equifax: 0990 783783

PO Box 30001
Glasgow G81 2DT

Index